get a grip on
ECOLOGY

Get a Grip on
ECOLOGY

DAVID BURNIE

WEIDENFELD
& NICOLSON

First published in the United Kingdom in 1999 by
Weidenfeld & Nicolson

A CIP catalogue record for this book is available from the
British Library

ISBN 0297 82702 2

This book was conceived, designed and produced by
The Ivy Press Limited, 2-3 St Andrews Place
Lewes, East Sussex BN7 1UP

Editorial Director: Sophie Collins
Art Director: Peter Bridgewater
Managing Editor: Anne Townley
Editor: Peter Leek
Designer: Angela English
Illustrations: Andrew Kulman
Picture Research: Vanessa Fletcher

Reproduction and Printing in Hong Kong by
Hong Kong Graphic and Printing Ltd.

Weidenfeld and Nicolson
Cassell & Co.
The Orion Publishing Group
Wellington House 125 Strand
London WC2R 0BB

CONTENTS

INTRODUCTION

WHAT IS ECOLOGY?

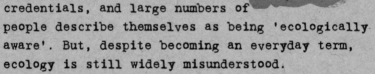

✱ Fifty years ago, few people had heard of ecology, and even fewer knew what the word meant. Just a few decades later, ecology has become a fashionable buzzword: consumer products proclaim their 'ecological' credentials, and large numbers of people describe themselves as being 'ecologically aware'. But, despite becoming an everyday term, ecology is still widely misunderstood.

A new science

Ernst Heinrich Haeckel (1834–1919) was one of Germany's most prominent naturalists in the 19th century, and an early supporter of the theory of evolution. He initially studied medicine, but developed an interest in marine biology, eventually becoming Professor of Zoology at the University of Jena. Haeckel was an accomplished artist, and made his name with a beautifully illustrated monograph on the Radiolaria – a group of single-celled planktonic organisms that are protected by glass-like skeletons made of silica.

Ernst Haeckel

EARLY BEGINNINGS

✱ The word ecology – or *Oecologie* in its German form – was coined by the naturalist **Ernst Haeckel** in 1866. He invented it by combining *oikos*, which is Greek for a home or household, with *logos*, another Greek word used to denote any kind of study. Taken literally, *ecology means the study of homes*.

✱ On the face of it, this may not seem to have much to do with the natural world. However, Haeckel's concept of the *oikos* was very much tied up with his interest in living things. During the mid-19th century, plants and animals were often studied in isolation, with little attention being paid to the way they related to their surroundings. Haeckel's new branch of biology was quite different. Instead of treating different species as isolated units, **Oecologie** *looked at the way they interacted* with their physical environment or 'household', and with the other species around them.

CHANGING GEAR

✷ During its early days, ecology rarely hit the headlines. Unlike chemists or physicists, ecologists worked with things that were difficult to measure, and many of their conclusions were hard to verify. But, despite these difficulties, ecological research gradually provoked a shift of thinking in biology. It showed that living things are linked in many subtle and unexpected ways, and that any disruption of these links can have major and often damaging results.

✷ In the second half of the 20th century, technological change and a rapidly expanding human population have disrupted natural systems to an extent never seen before. As a result, interest in ecology has exploded. After years in the shadows, it has become a key part of the science of life.

MARKET FORCES

What is the connection between ecology and economics? The answer – apart from a shared derivation from the Greek word *oikos* – is 'quite a lot'. Ecologists and economists often study the same topics, but in different contexts. These topics include resource availability, supply and demand, competition, and the costs involved in acquiring particular benefits. In the natural world, costs are paid in energy and resources, while in the human world they are paid in money.

what sort of habitat is this?

ecology is the study of natural environments

7

High life

The Scottish-born writer and naturalist **John Muir** (1838–1914) was one of America's earliest and most influential environmentalists. After studying at the University of Wisconsin, he took a job in a carriage repair shop, but was temporarily blinded by an accident. When he recovered, he gave up his work and began to explore the American continent, crossing much of it on foot. He fell in love with California's Sierra Nevada – 'the most divinely beautiful of all the mountain chains I have ever seen' – and became a passionate advocate of their preservation as a natural wilderness. Muir founded the <u>SIERRA CLUB</u> in 1892, and played a prominent part in persuading the US Government to adopt California's Yosemite Valley as a <u>NATIONAL PARK</u>.

IN TOUCH WITH THE EARTH

✱ Ecology and environmentalism are two different things. One is the scientific study of life in its natural environment; the other is the belief that the environment should be preserved and protected from man-made damage. In practice, the two are closely linked, because ecology provides information about how environmental damage affects living things, and how it might be put right.

THE SPORTING LIFE

✱ In the early days of ecology, concern about the environment was rare. Most naturalists – including Ernst Haeckel – thought nothing of shooting animals in order to study them. Collecting specimens was an almost obsessive activity, with thousands of birds, mammals and butterflies being pinned out, skinned or stuffed so they

killing animals so as to study them was not a problem to 19th-century naturalists

Mum, why aren't they moving?

could be put on display. On a trip to the Himalayas, one prominent plant collector, the British botanist **Sir Joseph Hooker**, got his Indian porters to ransack an area of forest for a particularly rare species of orchid. Not content with this destruction, he then told other orchid enthusiasts that it was an excellent way of making money.

collecting animal heads as trophies was a popular pastime

CONSERVE AND PRESERVE

✱ During the late 19th century, the tradition of treating wildlife as an inexhaustible resource continued, with big cats, buffalo and other animals being blasted towards oblivion. But by then it was becoming clear that there were some setbacks from which nature could not recover. One of these was the near-extinction of the American buffalo: its numbers collapsed from about ten million in 1800 to just over a thousand 80 years later.

✱ As the 20th century began, events like these helped to foster new attitudes towards the natural world. One was purely pragmatic: in order to exploit natural resources, they must sometimes be conserved. The second view – called PRESERVATIONISM – involved a more fundamental shift in thinking: the idea that nature has an intrinsic value, and should be protected simply for its own sake. Both these views form an important part of environmentalism today.

KEY WORDS

CONSERVATION: management of natural resources in a way that minimizes human impact

PRESERVATION: protection of living environments and their natural inhabitants by preventing human interference

you're driving me to extinction!

American buffalo

> 'It was a spring without voices. On the mornings that had once throbbed with the dawn chorus of robins, catbirds, doves, jays, wrens and scores of other bird voices there was now no sound; only silence lay over the fields and woods and marsh.'
> [from *Silent Spring*]

A WARNING VOICE

Rachel Carson (1907–64) was born in Pennsylvania. She studied marine biology, and later worked at the US Fish and Wildlife Service, initially as a scientific editor, and then as head of publications. In 1952 she completed *The Sea around Us*, a book that established her as a science writer. With the publication of *Silent Spring*, which followed ten years later, she was denounced by the chemical industry as a scaremonger – an accusation that she always strongly denied.

SILENT SPRING

* The modern environmental movement dates back to the early 1960s, with the publication of a best-selling book called *Silent Spring*. Written by Rachel Carson, an American naturalist and ecologist, it warned of a future world poisoned by synthetic pesticides, where birdsong was just a distant memory. At a time when established values were already under attack, Carson's book had a far-reaching impact.

ALARM CALL

caterpillar

* Rachel Carson wrote *Silent Spring* during a decade in which the long-term effects of new BIOCIDES were just starting to become apparent. One of the most widely used biocides, DDT, had proved extremely effective at eradicating insect pests, and had prevented the outbreak of serious insect-borne disease epidemics after the end of the Second World War.

* Unfortunately, events showed that DDT harmed a wide range of animals in addition to the ones it was intended to kill. In some cases, death was caused by direct poisoning, but, in others, DDT did

DDT was indiscriminate in
its destructive effects

its damage in a more roundabout way.
Pelicans and falcons, for example, failed
to breed because DDT prevented them
forming normal eggshells. When the
birds settled down to incubate their
eggs, the fragile shells broke, killing
entire broods in a matter of moments.

so that
was the
reason

DDT

NO HIDING PLACE

✱ *Silent Spring* helped to
publicize the specific threats
posed by organic pesticides,
but it also revealed a disturbing
shift in the way human activities affect the
environment. Until the 20th century,
pollution was largely a regional
phenomenon: anything distant from cities
and factories was likely to be distant from
pollutants as well. But, with the
development of chemicals such as DDT,
this regional link was broken. ***DDT proved
to be remarkably*** PERSISTENT***, and easily
shuttled between soil, air, water and living
things.*** In a handful of years, this
combination of characteristics allowed it to
spread from farmland to the open oceans
and even to Antarctica.

✱ *Rachel Carson's work showed that the
environment cannot be divided into self-
contained compartments.* Today, action to
protect the environment involves the entire
BIOSPHERE – the complete range of settings
in which living things are found.

DDT

DDT belongs to a family
of chemicals known as
CHLORINATED
HYDROCARBONS. It was
originally synthesized in
1873, but its insect-killing
powers were not discovered
until 1939, by the Swiss
chemist **Paul Müller**.

KEY WORDS

BIOCIDE:
any chemical used to
kill plant or animal
pests
ORGANIC:
in chemistry, an organic
compound is one that
contains carbon. It may
be natural or man-
made. The same word
is also used in a
different context to
describe food that has
been produced without
the use of synthetic
biocides or fertilizers.

11

ecologists look at every
aspect of living things

INTRODUCING THE BIOSPHERE

* It's possible to be a pure mathematician, but quite impossible to be a pure ecologist. This is because ecology probes complex interactions between the living and non-living worlds, and draws on many other sciences in the course of its research. One thing binds these interactions together: they all take place within the biosphere - the sum-total of all the places where living organisms can be found.

LIFE INSIDE THE EARTH

Experimental drilling has shown that bacteria can survive in rock pores at depths of nearly 3km (2 miles). The main factor limiting their depth is heat, which increases the deeper you go. Under the sea, where the temperature rise is more gradual than on land, some bacteria may be able to survive at depths of up to 7km (4.5 miles).

LIFE'S FUZZY LIMITS

* If you imagine a sheet of cling-film wrapped around a football, you will have some idea of the thickness of the biosphere compared with the rest of the planet. The biosphere's thinness is due to the fact that living things need liquid water, and they can only survive within a set range of temperatures. This means that Earth's outer atmosphere and planetary core are strictly off-limits.

* However, in any one place, the precise boundaries of the biosphere are difficult to pin down. At one time, life on Earth was thought to be a largely superficial business, with almost all living things clustered at or near the surface. However, in recent years it has become clear that microbes sometimes drift high into the air, while bacteria have been discovered in porous rocks several kilometres underground, expanding the biosphere even further.

DIVERSIONARY TACTICS

* Even if life didn't exist on Earth, energy from inside and outside the planet would keep matter on the move. But, in the biosphere, the presence of life makes things much more complex. Living things siphon off some of the energy around them, and use it for their own needs. This energy drives a set of <u>BIOGEOCHEMICAL CYCLES</u> that shuttle materials between the interlinked worlds of living and non-living matter.

* *In energy terms, planet Earth is an open system, because it receives energy from space, and it also radiates it back again.* However, as far as life's raw materials are concerned, Earth is a tightly closed system. This means that living things cannot work like a mining company, exhausting reserves in one area and then moving on to another. Instead, they have to constantly recycle the stockpile of available materials. This recycling has created the interlocking processes that shape the whole of life on Earth.

the biosphere is a thin layer around the Earth

Alternative Earth

In 1991, a team of eight scientists took up residence in *'Biosphere 2'* – a self-contained 'world' built in the Sonoran Desert. Covering over 1 hectare (2.5 acres), the complex of glasshouses and accommodation units contained selected food plants and animals, living in an atmosphere humidified by a miniature 'ocean'. After a promising start, this long-term experiment – initially scheduled to run for two years – started to come adrift as carbon dioxide levels began to rise and crop plants were attacked by pests. The team of 'biospherians' emerged from the experience in relatively good health, but they had demonstrated the difficulties involved in creating a permanently balanced system.

MATTER ON THE MOVE

✳ Just over 90 chemical elements occur naturally on Earth. Of these, only about two dozen are essential for life. These elements constantly cycle through living and non-living matter, following pathways known as BIOGEOCHEMICAL CYCLES. Some parts of these cycles are over in a split second, while others take millions of years.

Not so vital

At one time, chemists believed that the substances in living things contained a 'vital force', making them fundamentally different from the chemicals in non-living matter. This doctrine – called VITALISM – took a severe knock in 1828 when the German chemist **Friedrich Wöhler** managed to make urea, a substance found in urine, from ammonium cyanate, an inorganic salt. By the 1860s, chemists had found out how to SYNTHESIZE many organic chemicals from simple inorganic substances.

Friedrich Wöhler

there are four important elements that living things need

HYDROGEN OXYGEN NITROGEN CARBON

THE CARBON KEY

✳ Life's essential elements are a highly mixed bag. They include metals such as iron, copper, chromium and zinc, together with non-metals such as sulphur, chlorine and iodine. *Living things use only minute quantities of most of them, but they need four in large amounts. The 'big four' include three gases – hydrogen, oxygen and nitrogen – and carbon, the element that is the key to life.*

✳ The Earth's supply of carbon is partitioned into four different stores – the planet's crust, the sea, the atmosphere,

the essential
elements of life
are a mixed bag

and living things. The crust has by far the biggest share of this stockpile, while the atmosphere has the smallest, weighing in at a mere 650 billion tonnes. Plants soak up carbon dioxide from the air as they grow, and animals replace it as they breathe. Together, they manage to turn over the atmosphere's entire supply of carbon roughly once every 4.5 years.

LENGTHY DIVERSION

* When an animal breathes, carbon is shuttled almost instantly from one part of the carbon cycle to another. But, when the remains of living things get buried, their carbon can be transformed into fossil fuels, locking it out of the rest of the cycle for immense periods of time. This store of carbon is like a bank account that has seen far more money coming in than going out for millions of years. As a result, it contains far more carbon than in everything alive today.

* That, at least, is how things stood before human beings became involved. *By burning fossil fuels we have stepped up the flow of carbon from the Earth's crust back into the air, pumping it from the largest carbon store into the smallest. This process has rapidly accelerated in the last 200 years, and – as we will see later – the results are beginning to show.*

pumping carbon
into the air

BIOGEOCHEMICAL CYCLE:
the cyclical movement of any element through the atmosphere, the oceans, the Earth's crust and living things

WHY CARBON?

Carbon dominates the chemistry of life. This is because its atoms are unusually good at linking up, not only with themselves, but also with the atoms of other elements. As a result, carbon can form millions of different molecules, all with different chemical properties.

15

SOMETHING IN THE AIR

✱ In Samuel Taylor Coleridge's famous poem *The Rime of the Ancient Mariner*, the crewmen of a doomed ship are tortured by thirst while an ocean of water stretches all around them. If you swap water for nitrogen, you have some idea of the situation facing plants and animals as they try to get hold of a crucially important element.

Perfect partners

Many plants harbour nitrogen-fixing bacteria, but peas and their relatives are outstandingly good at welcoming them on board. Known collectively as legumes, these plants fertilize the soil by adding nitrogen to it as they grow, and also after they die. As long ago as the third century BC, the Greek philosopher **Theophrastus** recorded how legumes were used to improve soil fertility. Despite the advent of artificial fertilizers, legumes are still grown for exactly the same reason today.

even large animals depend on the bacteria fixers for their nitrogen

peas are good at welcoming nitrogen-fixing bacteria

ONLY THE LOWLY

✱ Nitrogen is an essential ingredient of <u>PROTEINS AND NUCLEIC ACIDS</u> – large and highly complex molecules found in all living things. It makes up about four-fifths of the atmosphere, so it is never in short supply. However, it's a remarkable fact of life that plants and animals have never evolved ways to exploit nitrogen directly. Instead, they can use it only after it has been 'fixed', or converted into nitrogen compounds.

✱ One way nitrogen gets fixed is by being roasted by lightning. A quick jolt raises the air temperature by thousands of degrees, providing enough energy to make nitrogen and oxygen combine. Rain then washes nitrogen compounds into the soil. But for life generally, the most important NITROGEN FIXERS by far are a small group of highly specialized bacteria. Without them, usable nitrogen would disappear, and most of life would come to a halt.

PAYING GUESTS

* These key players in the nitrogen cycle live in two different ways. Some exist independently in soil or in water, but most live in partnership with plants, growing on or inside their roots. The bacteria provide their plant hosts with nitrogen in a form they can use, and in return their hosts supply the bacteria with energy-rich food, and a secure environment. When animals eat plants, the nitrogen is handed on.

nitrogen works wonders

* In many parts of the world, a shortage of usable nitrogen is one of the main factors that holds back the growth of plants; the other being a shortage of phosphorus. As farmers and ecologists have discovered, when one of these LIMITING FACTORS is suddenly removed – for example *by adding artificial fertilizer – the results can be spectacular. However, as we will see later, using fertilizers can also create environmental\problems that are difficult to solve.*

adding artificial fertilizers can have dramatic results

roots

vegetable

17

it's OK, there's enough water to go round

FLUID APPROACH

✱ At some point, all biogeochemical cycles involve water, because water forms the fluid environment inside all living things. But water also moves in a cycle of its own. Every year, half a billion cubic kilometres of sea water evaporate into the air, creating the rain that allows land-based life to survive.

all living things
need water to survive

Life-giving impurities

In the natural world, pure water is rare. Even in the most pristine conditions, rainwater contains dissolved substances, such as nitrates that have been created by lightning. Some forms of life – including plants that grow high up in trees – depend on these dissolved chemicals as a source of nutrients.

water

needing to replace water every day

THE MEDIUM OF LIFE

✱ Compared with the total amount of water involved in the water cycle, the proportion held in living matter is tiny. For example, the water in the world's entire human population adds up to about 200 million cubic metres (7 billion cubic feet) – roughly the amount that flows down the Amazon every 20 minutes. But compared with nitrogen and many other elements, water doesn't stay around for long once it has found its way into living tissue. Most living things replace a significant amount of their water every day, and the smaller they are, the faster this turnover takes place. As a result, the total amount of water flowing through living things is surprisingly high.

TURNING ON THE TAPS

✱ This paradoxical fact means that, simply by being alive, living things can sometimes have a substantial impact on local parts of the water cycle. A camel or a cactus doesn't have much effect on the water cycle in a desert, because the total weight of animal and plant life in deserts is small. But in a forest, where the total weight of living things is much greater, their effect on the water is much more pronounced. Forests act like living sponges, mopping up rain after it falls and then releasing it back into the air as water vapour. A big forest can do this on such a large scale that it shapes the local climate.

I haven't got a problem

✱ *When humans come into the picture, the impact on the water cycle is even bigger. This is because we use water for agriculture and industry as well as for simply staying alive. In developed countries, this extra water exceeds human biological needs hundreds of times over, which explains why – in a planet awash with water – our impact on the water cycle is now felt world-wide.*

human beings use water for lots of things apart from just staying alive

---

ANCIENT WATER

Once water has fallen as rain, it has two ways of getting back to the sea – either over the ground, or through it. *Compared with the surface water, ground water often flows very slowly, sometimes moving less than a metre (3ft) in a year.* In some parts of the world, such as the High Plains states of the USA, the underlying rock contains 'fossil' water from rain that fell thousands of years ago.

ENERGY AND ORDER

first you see it, then you don't

* Imagine a sugar cube putting itself back together once it has dissolved. It's not impossible, but the chances of it happening are almost infinitely small. But, with living things, 'impossible' processes like this seem to happen all the time. This is because living organisms - unlike all other kinds of matter - can use energy to become increasingly ordered as time goes by.

don't break the rules

Hidden reserves

All living things build up energy stores that can tide them over periods when their external energy supply temporarily comes to a halt. Diatoms, for example, contain tiny globules of energy-rich oil. This helps them to float, and also acts as a fuel during the hours of darkness. In plants, the energy store is often in the form of sugar or starch, while, in animals, body fat acts as a fuel when food is hard to find.

diatom

BREAKING THE RULE

* Microscopic organisms called diatoms show how far-reaching some of these processes can be. Diatoms live in water, and they support themselves by making ornate cases from silica, the mineral we use to make glass. In water, silica levels are often very low – just a few parts per million – which is vastly lower than sugar levels in a cup of coffee. Nevertheless, diatoms manage to scavenge what silica there is and fashion it in highly complex ways.

* On the face of it, this process seems to break an important physical principle – the *second law of thermodynamics*. This law

states that whenever energy is passed on or transformed, some of it always changes into a form that cannot be used. As a result, disorder always tends to increase. Put in physical terms, the system's ENTROPY goes up.

DRIVING FORCE

✱ Physical laws apply to all forms of matter, so how do diatoms – and other living things – manage to turn this law on its head? The answer is that they don't. Taken in isolation, a diatom certainly becomes more ordered as it develops, but that is only part of the story. Looked at as a whole, diatoms and their environment become more disordered as time goes by, because energy and raw materials eventually become more *but it's broken the second rule* dispersed. Diatoms can *of thermodynamics* continue to grow and reproduce only because new supplies of energy arrive all the time, in the form of sunlight. If that supply of energy is cut off, the diatoms quickly die and disorder soon ensues.

✱ What is true of diatoms is also true of all living things, regardless of the energy source they use. *Life is like a machine: without a constant supply of energy it eventually comes to a halt.*

KEY WORDS

ENTROPY:
a measure of the amount of disorder in any physical system. In a closed system, entropy either remains constant or increases. In an open system, including ones involving living things, entropy can decrease, but only on a local scale.

A death foretold

The second law of thermodynamics has one disconcerting implication: given enough time, the universe will eventually reach a point at which there will be no available energy left to do any form of work.

Fortunately for us, this gloomy scenario – known as the heat death of the universe – is billions of years off.

LIVING ON LIGHT

* Every year, the earth receives enough solar energy to keep the human race going for about 30,000 years. A tiny fraction of this energy - just one per cent - is intercepted by plants, creating the first link in an ecological pass-the-parcel game that powers most of life.

I've got enough energy left for another 30,000 years

LIGHT WORK

* Plants harness solar energy through the process of photosynthesis, which means *'putting together by light'*. The chemistry of photosynthesis is hugely complicated, but the end result is simple: two inorganic substances – carbon dioxide from the air and water from the soil – combine to become energy-packed organic compounds. These compounds make up plant tissues and fuel plant growth, and their energy is handed on when plants are eaten.

LIFE AT THE LIMITS

The record depth for photosynthetic life in the sea is 268m (879ft). At this depth, the organism in question – a form of red alga found off the Bahamas – ekes out a living on light that is less than a thousandth as strong as the daylight at the surface.

How do they do that?

Until three centuries ago, people assumed that plants lived by 'eating' nutrients in the soil. This idea suffered its first real setback with one of the earliest quantitative experiments in biology, carried out by the Belgian physician **Jan Baptista van Helmont** (1577–1644). Van Helmont grew a sapling in a pot, and after five years measured the change in weight of the sapling and of the soil. The sapling's weight went up by over 70kg (154lb), but the soil's weight decreased by less than 60g (2oz).

✳ Plants were not the first organisms to develop photosynthesis, but they have become by far the most important practitioners of this way of life. Plants generate about 100 billion tonnes of energy-rich compounds a year – food that ultimately fuels most of life on Earth.

SECOND-HAND FOOD

✳ In energy terms, photosynthesis makes plants completely self-sufficient. To survive, all they need is light and a supply of simple raw materials. Most other forms of life – including animals – are quite different, because they obtain energy by breaking down organic matter. Without something to make organic matter in the first place, they could not exist. This fundamental difference divides the living world into two camps, known as <u>AUTOTROPHS</u> and <u>HETEROTROPHS</u>. Autotrophs collect energy directly, while heterotrophs pick it up second-hand, either from autotrophs or from each other.

LIFE IN THE DARK

✳ There are a few environments on Earth where life does not ultimately depend on light. In sea-floor volcanic vents, caves and hot springs, some bacteria obtain their energy and raw materials directly from chemicals dissolved in water. If the sun suddenly stopped shining, these primitive organisms would be the only living things that could survive.

KEY WORDS

PHOTOSYNTHESIS:
the conversion of light energy into chemical energy by living things. In plants, light energy is collected by chlorophyll, a green pigment in leaves.

AUTOTROPH:
an organism that can make all the organic substances that it needs by collecting energy and simple raw materials from its surroundings. Autotrophs include plants, algae and some bacteria.

HETEROTROPH:
an organism that uses existing organic matter as a source of energy and raw materials. Heterotrophs include all animals and fungi, together with many bacteria and other micro-organisms.

23

SOAKING UP THE SUN

* Asked which is the more productive, a swamp or a piece of farmland, most people will go for the farmland. However, the answer depends on exactly what 'productive' means. To an ecologist, swamps often win, because they can turn sunlight into living matter at a record-breaking rate.

swamps are more fertile than farmland

NUTRIENTS DOWN THE DRAIN

Productivity is often low in the oceans because most organisms sink to the bottom when they die. This means there is a constant drain of nutrients from the sunlit surface layers, where all the primary production has to take place. The exceptions to this rule are places where currents flow upwards from the sea bed, bringing nutrients with them. These currents explain the rich sea life off the west coasts of southern Africa and South America.

THE PRODUCTIVITY STAKES

* In ecology, <u>PRODUCTIVITY</u> measures *the rate at which new living matter is created* when plants harness energy from the Sun. In the course of a year, a square metre of an average swamp puts on about 2.5kg (5.5lb) of extra plant growth, while the same area of a tropical rainforest manages about 2kg (4.4lb). Compared with this, cultivated land often trails way behind. Although it is productive in terms of human food, its biological productivity averages only about 0.65kg (1.4lb) per square metre – only slightly ahead of natural grassland.

✱ In ecology, <u>PRIMARY PRODUCTIVITY</u> is a key figure, because it shows how fast energy is channelled through living things. We currently use up about 40% of the Earth's primary productivity – by eating food, farming animals, and cutting down trees – meaning that only 60% is now left for the wild species that also use it for survival.

PILE 'EM HIGH

✱ High productivity doesn't necessarily mean that an ecosystem is piled high with plants, because, as new plants grow, old ones decay. Also, living plants tie up energy for different lengths of time. As a result, some ecosystems shoulder an immense weight of plants, while others have very little.

✱ This total weight is known as the <u>PLANT BIOMASS</u>. On land, tropical rainforests top the biomass charts, with up to 45,000 tonnes of plant life crammed onto every square kilometre of ground. Swamps have about 15,000 tonnes, while deserts have less than 1,000. But, in the open oceans, life is far more thinly spread. Here, micro-organisms take the place of plants, and they average about 3 tonnes per square kilometre – a mere scattering adrift in the vastness of the sea.

tropical rainforest

KEY WORDS

PRODUCTIVITY:
the rate at which energy is built into living matter. **Primary Productivity** shows the rate at which photosynthetic organisms – usually plants – capture energy from sunlight, while **Secondary Productivity** is the rate at which animals build themselves up from plants.
BIOMASS:
the combined weight of living things in any place. The water in plants and animals is usually excluded.

Energy in transit

In the 1970s, two ecologists – **R. H. Whittaker** and **G. E. Likens** – worked out how long energy stays locked up in living plants. In tropical rainforests, the figure is about 22.5 years, while in grassland it is about 3 years. For the micro-organisms that live in water, the times are much shorter because most of these organisms are eaten after a few days.

living things each
have a place within
the energy chain

LIFE ON THE LEVEL

* When a deer browses on
the leaves of a tree, it
carries off energy the
tree has collected
directly from the Sun.
But when a wolf attacks
its prey, the energy it
collects may have been
through three or four other
living things already. Differences
like these allow living things to be slotted into
separate 'trophic levels', according to their
position in the energy chain.

that fat pig is
not going to
eat me

Multi-level consumers

Instead of fitting into a
single trophic level, some
consumers slot into
several different levels.
Humans are a prime case.
You, for example, are a
first-order consumer if
you eat an apple, but a
second-order consumer if
you eat a beefburger.
If you have a liking
for fish, this can
elevate you to the
status of third- or
even fourth-order
consumer, because
the chances are that
the fish got its
energy at second
or third hand.

A STEP UP

* In living systems, the lowest trophic
level is always made up of <u>PRODUCERS</u> —
forms of life that carry out the essential
first step of capturing energy and building
it into organic matter. On land, producers
are almost invariably plants, but in water
they include a vast array of simpler
and much smaller
organisms, such as diatoms
and other algae. These
floating producers are
too small to be seen with
the naked eye, but taken
together they account for
a large proportion of the
total energy living things
collect from the Sun.

shall I be a first-order
consumer or a second-
order consumer?

✱ The next trophic level consists of first-order <u>CONSUMERS</u>. These eat food created by the producers, and they in turn are eaten by second-order consumers, which may then be eaten by third-order consumers. But at this point the energy chain often comes to a halt. Fourth-order consumers – the super-predators of the living world – are very rare.

this second-order consumer sure tastes good

FIZZLING OUT

✱ The reason why the energy chain comes to an end is that at each step up the chain only a small proportion of the energy that is handed on ends up being built into living matter. The remainder – up to nine-tenths in some cases – is used as fuel, to make the animals' bodies work. This energy escapes to the environment, often in the form of heat, and so it cannot be passed on.

✱ *This step-by-step loss means that for a consumer the best way of collecting energy is to cut out the middleman and eat producers directly*. This explains why most of the world's largest animals are not hunters, but species that feed on plants. It also explains why 'top predators', such as lions and sharks, tend to be thinly spread.

Chilling out

In terms of energy efficiency, cold-blooded animals are better than warm-blooded ones at making the most of their food. This is because they do not need to use up lots of heat energy simply keeping their bodies warm. However, there is a payback for being warm-blooded: a warm body temperature allows animals to stay active whatever the conditions around them, which increases their chances of finding a meal.

there could be a
million in here

CHAINS AND WEBS

* In the early 1920s, a British ecologist called Charles Elton drew up a chart that linked all the plants and animals in a small area of windswept Arctic tundra, according to what ate what. It was a painstaking job, but it established a concept that has since become a key part of ecology.

earthworms feed on the dead remains of other organisms

Living on leftovers

An important part of any food web consists of DECOMPOSERS – living things that feed on the dead remains of other organisms. Decomposers (sometimes called DETRITIVORES) include small animals such as insects and earthworms, but the last stages in the breakdown process are carried out by micro-scopic fungi and bacteria. A single cubic centimetre of soil can contain over ten million of them.

INVISIBLE LINKS

* In nature, food has to come from somewhere. By tracing it up and down the different trophic levels, it is possible to see what makes it in the first place, and where it eventually ends up. The result is a FOOD CHAIN – a route map of the path taken by food energy as it passes through different species.

* Even in a bleak place like the Arctic tundra there are dozens of species of animals and plants. At first glance this makes it seem quite likely that food chains here might be 10 or 20 links long. But, because energy is lost every time food is handed on, food chains are much shorter than this. Half a dozen links is good going; many chains have just two or three.

KEY WORDS

FOOD CHAIN:
a food pathway that connects one species with another
FOOD WEB:
a collection of interlinked food chains

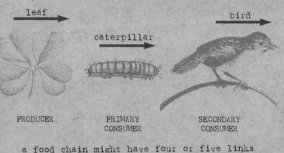

leaf

caterpillar

bird

cat

PRODUCER

PRIMARY
CONSUMER

SECONDARY
CONSUMER

TERTIARY
CONSUMER

a food chain might have four or five links

JOIN THE DOTS

✱ Although individual food chains are short, there are usually many of them. Taken together they form a food web – a network of criss-crossing lines that often looks like a subway plan. If the web is complete (something that isn't easy to achieve), it shows all the possible routes that food can follow in an entire community of plants and animals. In a typical food web, some animals are connected by only a few lines, while others are on major intersections. This is either because they have wide-ranging diets, or because they have the misfortune to feature on many predators' menus.

✱ Working out food webs can be an interesting task – particularly when it has to be done in far-flung parts of the world. But food webs aren't simply a record of the status quo. Because they show how species are linked, they can be used to predict the knock-on effects when habitats are polluted, and when one species declines or dies out.

Charles Elton

SHIFTING WITH THE SEASONS

Most food webs – particularly ones based on land – are snapshots of what eats what at a particular time of year. Seasonal changes can transform food webs, particularly in winter when plants die down, some animals hibernate, and others migrate.

Travelling traces

In the 1920s, **Charles Elton** worked out his tundra food web by watching what the various animals ate. Today, webs are often put together by 'labelling' plants with small amounts of a harmless radioactive isotope. The isotope is then tracked as it passes through different animals.

CHAOS AND COMPLEXITY

✱ Food chains and food webs show that in the natural world there is no such thing as being completely alone. Even in the most inaccessible habitats, living things influence each other, and also interact with their surroundings. Many of these interactions are so complex that, no matter how intensively they are studied, their outcome can never be predicted.

The butterfly effect

Chaos theory was developed in the 1960s by the meteorologist **Edward Lorenz**. He showed that it was impossible to predict the exact path followed by rising air, even though its overall movement could be foretold. Lorenz also showed that, in theory, any tiny perturbation – for example the flapping of a butterfly's wings – could have a knock-on effect out of all proportion to its size. The 'butterfly effect' has since become a metaphor for the interconnectedness of the biosphere as a whole.

it's total chaos

nature is much messier than a game of snooker

UNPREDICTABLE EVENTS

✱ In a game of snooker or pool, things work in a foreseeable way. In theory, if you could gather enough data it would be possible to predict exactly where each ball would end up after it had been hit. In nature, things are fundamentally different. Even with enough data to fill all the computer memories on earth, it would still be impossible to predict the future course of a system involving living things. The overall picture is foreseeable, but the fine detail is not.

✱ *Systems like this are said to be chaotic.* However, chaotic systems don't necessarily feature living things:

they also include a host of physical phenomena on many different scales, from the movement of grains in a pile of sand to the circulation of air and water over the whole of the Earth.

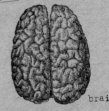

it's getting too hot in here

brain

STAYING ON COURSE

✷ Chaos makes it sound as if life is a muddled business, full of sudden changes of direction. However, this isn't what ecologists see as they examine the natural world. The day-to-day detail of living systems often fluctuates, but, over the longer term, continuity is usually the order of the day.

✷ *So what is it that keeps chaos under control? One factor is that living things have built-in constraints.* A tree, for example, can't suddenly develop a new way of reproducing, any more than an elephant can take up life in the sea. But a more far-reaching factor is that control is an integral feature of life. Through a process called feedback, living things maintain the steady conditions they need to survive. However, feedback systems have their limits. How far they can be pushed without them breaking down is one of the most urgent questions confronting ecologists today.

FEEDBACK

A feedback system is one that automatically reacts to change. The most common kind involves NEGATIVE FEEDBACK, which reverses any drift away from an optimum state. Human body temperature is controlled by negative feedback. As soon as the body's temperature begins to rise or fall, sensors in the brain detect the change. The brain then activates processes that bring the body temperature back to its normal level. POSITIVE FEEDBACK has the opposite effect: it reinforces the change.

animals live the kind of life to which they are adapted

31

THE GAIA HYPOTHESIS

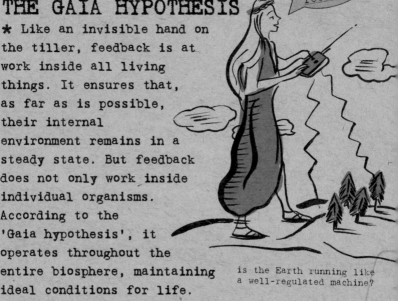

I think I'm getting some feedback

* Like an invisible hand on the tiller, feedback is at work inside all living things. It ensures that, as far as is possible, their internal environment remains in a steady state. But feedback does not only work inside individual organisms. According to the 'Gaia hypothesis', it operates throughout the entire biosphere, maintaining ideal conditions for life.

is the Earth running like a well-regulated machine?

BREATHING FREE

Until about two billion years ago, the Earth's atmosphere contained no oxygen. Oxygen did not appear until micro-organisms started to live by photosynthesis, releasing the gas as a by-product. Since then, the atmosphere's oxygen level has risen to its present level of about 21%. This is high enough to support oxygen-breathing life, but not so high that land-based life runs a serious risk of catching fire.

OUR SELF-REGULATING EARTH

* There is no doubt that, in the world as a whole, some feedback mechanisms operate on the grandest of scales. For example, if the amount of carbon dioxide in the atmosphere rises, plant growth speeds up. The growing plants remove more carbon from the air, helping to check the carbon dioxide rise. In a similar way, if the Earth's temperature increases, plants give off more water vapour. This boosts the amount of cloud cover, putting a brake on the temperature rise. Thanks to photosynthesis (pages 22–3), the entire composition of the atmosphere is the way it is *only because life exists on Earth*.

✱ In the 1970s, facts like these convinced **James Lovelock**, a British chemist and engineer, that the biosphere works like a single integrated system, optimizing conditions for living things. He developed this idea with the American biologist **Lynn Margulis**, and called it the Gaia hypothesis, after the Earth goddess of the ancient Greeks. According to the hypothesis, the living world is like an enormous self-regulating machine, constantly making the adjustments needed to maintain a steady state.

IS GAIA REAL?

✱ From the moment it was first floated, the Gaia hypothesis has been controversial. Lovelock and Margulis have identified a range of feedback mechanisms that seem to back it up, but opponents of the idea have found plenty that work in the opposite direction. A trickier problem is that the Gaia hypothesis suggests some kind of global cooperation among living things – something that runs counter to the Darwinian idea of a struggle for existence. The notion of competing organisms working together to maintain equilibrum has led many ecologists view Gaia with scepticism.

✱ *Despite this mixed reception, the Gaia hypothesis has proved to be a valuable piece of speculation. Even if the biosphere is not really a single entity, it sometimes behaves uncannily like one.*

Claude Bernard

Steady as she goes

The idea that living things maintain a stable internal state was first put forward in the 19th century, by the French physiologist **Claude Bernard** (1813–78). In the 20th century, the American physiologist **Walter Cannon** gave Bernard's concept a name: homeostasis, which literally means 'standing still'. Homeostasis is essential for life. This is because the chemical reactions involved in staying alive work best only in a narrow range of conditions.

Walter Cannon

CHAPTER 1

NO PLACE LIKE HOME

* Taken as a whole, the biosphere is a daunting subject to study. It is home to perhaps 30 million species of living things, and an endless tangle of interactions. Fortunately, this tangle can be broken down into simpler parts. Known as ecosystems, these are the ecological equivalent of neighbourhoods, complete with all their inhabitants.

you must watch no. 36 – they'll barbecue anything and anyone

the residents of an ecosystem are not always friendly

Living homes

Some ecosystems are set in living surroundings. The lining of a human mouth, for example, is home to dozens of species of bacteria, while over 300 kinds have been identified on teeth. These micro-organisms make up part of the body's normal 'bacterial flora', and they create their own food webs fuelled by substances that we eat. Most of them are quite harmless. One that isn't is *Streptococcus mutans*, a bacterium involved in tooth decay.

NEIGHBOURS AT WAR

* Ecosystems consist of two basic ingredients – living things, and the surroundings that form their collective home. Like human neighbourhoods, they don't have a set size: an ecosystem can be as small as a puddle or as large as an entire forest. In ecological jargon, the residents of the *ecosystem make up a 'community'* – a characteristic collection of living things which exchange energy and nutrients with their surroundings, and also with each other.

* Despite its homely sound, an ecological community doesn't imply friendly relations, because exchanging nutrients with your neighbours often involves catching and eating them.

over 300 species of bacteria have been identified on teeth

MOVING ON

✳ For convenience, ecosystems are often treated as if they were closed and separate units. In reality, nature is not nearly this clear-cut. Many ecosystems have blurred boundary zones where they merge with others around them, and, although all have their collection of permanent residents, most also host species that regularly come and go. Many of these part-timers are MIGRANTS – animals that move in at a particular time of year, when the ecosystem has most to offer. When conditions change and things aren't so congenial, they go elsewhere.

✳ As well as these temporary residents, there are species that divide up their time in a different way. Animals that undergo METAMORPHOSIS – such as frogs, butterflies and barnacles – often spend the first part of their lives in one ecosystem, and their adult lives in another. By changing shape, they can exploit one source of food when they are young, and a quite different one when they are adult. More importantly, changing shape helps them to spread – something that all species do to maximize their chances of survival.

animals like frogs change shape so as to improve their chances of survival

KEY WORDS

MIGRATION:
a seasonal movement to a more favourable environment

METAMORPHOSIS:
a gradual or abrupt change in body shape, producing adult organisms that look quite different from their young

I think I'll start with this ecosystem

NEW IDEA - NEW NAME

Like many concepts in ecology, ecosystems are a relatively new idea. The word was first coined in 1936, by the British plant ecologist **A. G. Tansley.**

35

FITTING IN

* In any ecosystem, living things aren't scattered about at random. Instead, each species has a preferred habitat - a part of the ecosystem that suits it best. Some species are fairly flexible, and can cope with a range of different habitats, but most are much more choosy. Without the right set of conditions, they cannot survive.

each species
has its place

The multidimensional niche

In the late 1950s, the ecologist **G. Evelyn Hutchinson** put the idea of niches into a mathematical form by treating every factor in the environment as a separate dimension in space. If a species has three basic requirements, for example, the ranges that bound its niche make up a volume in three dimensions. If it has ten requirements, they make up a ten-dimensional space. Although spaces like this cannot be visualized, they can be used to build up a statistical profile of a species.

THE 'MUST-HAVE' MINERAL

* This choosiness is almost always due to specific physical needs. For example, freshwater crayfish – relatives of crabs and lobsters – build their body cases out of calcium carbonate, a mineral they collect from water. They thrive in rivers and streams

crayfish

where the water is hard, because hard water is rich in dissolved calcium. Soft-water rivers, on the other hand, are bad news. They may teem with food, but as far as crayfish are concerned, their lack of calcium puts them strictly out of bounds.

crab

✱ This is just one of a host of factors that can dictate where individual species live. Others include temperature, humidity and oxygen levels, the acidity of the soil or the amount of sunshine or shade. In any one place, it is rare for every factor to be just right, but if just one falls outside a species' tolerance limits, that species will not succeed there.

KEY WORDS

HABITAT:
the place where a plant or animal lives
NICHE:
the place and role of a species within an ecosystem

FINDING A NICHE

watch the nematodes

✱ If you think of an ecosystem as a neighbourhood, a habitat is an address. Different species often share the same address, but they never share precisely the same way of life. In ecological terms, **each has a separate 'niche'.** An ecological niche is far more than the place where something lives: it sums up the way a species functions in the ecosystem, and includes not only its habitat, but its entire way of life.

✱ Niches have important implications in wildlife conservation because, unlike humans, animals and plants cannot choose to change the way they live. If just one of their niche requirements isn't met – even though all the rest are exactly right – the chances are that they will fail to thrive, and there's a danger that they may even disappear altogether.

STRANGE HABITATS

Quite by accident, humans sometimes create habitats that turn out to be just right for living things. One of the most bizarre must be the damp beer-mat. A species of nematode, or roundworm, seems to revel in these flat and intoxicating surroundings, but is rarely encountered in the wild.

37

GENERALISTS AND SPECIALISTS

* Why are some species so picky about how and where they live, while others seem to be much less fussy? The answer lies in natural selection - the driving force behind evolution.

Generalists exploit a wide range of opportunities, but specialists concentrate on just a few - sometimes to much better effect.

Natural selection

Natural selection was first identified by the English naturalist Charles Darwin, who described it in his ground-breaking book *On the Origin of Species*. It is the process that favours the best-adapted individuals in any group, ensuring that they leave the most offspring. As a result, their characteristics become more common, making the group evolve. Natural selection is responsible for practically all the adaptations seen in living things, including their ecological relationships.

I'm quite happy here!

some species will live anywhere

FOCUS GROUPS

* In ecological terms, a generalist is a species with a wide niche. These species sound as if they should always do better than specialists, because they can use a wide range of resources. As a result, they should produce lots of offspring, which is *the hallmark of biological success*.

* To some extent, this is true. However, there is another side to this coin. Generalists – such as racoons, crows and starlings – are the jacks-of-all-trades of the living world. Although they can exploit many kinds of food, they are not ideally qualified to make the most of any single one. By contrast, a

racoon

GENERALISTS exploit many kinds of food

crow

species that focuses on a particular food is likely to be very good at dealing with it. Up to a point, the more specialized a species is, the greater that advantage becomes.

STRIKING A BALANCE

* This drive towards specialization is one of the recurring themes of evolution, and in some cases it is taken to remarkable lengths. For example, the aardwolf – an African member of the dog family – sometimes eats small mammals and birds, but its main food consists of termites, which its laps up with its sticky tongue. The giant panda is stranger still. Its direct ancestors are carnivores, but it lives entirely on bamboo.

the drive towards specialization

not bamboo again, mum

giant pandas only eat bamboo

* If a key resource is plentiful, a species that specializes in using it can reap rich rewards. *However, as the giant panda all too clearly shows, there is a risk attached to this way of life: specialization is difficult to undo. When humans alter habitats, and food supplies begin to shrink, specialists are first onto the list of casualties.*

FEATHER BEDDING

Parasites called feather lice are among the world's greatest ecological specialists. They suck the blood of birds, but they don't simply attack any bird that happens to come along. Each species of louse feeds on a particular host species, and will rarely thrive on any other. The match between parasite and host is so precise that bird evolution can be pieced together by examining lice instead of birds.

39

Sorry: fully booked

Biodiversity seems to have a natural tendency to increase, unless some kind of setback puts it into reverse. However, ecologists are unsure if it keeps on climbing in any given ecosystem, or if it eventually reaches a plateau, at which point the ecosystem in question is full. In both situations, new species appear and old ones become extinct, but, in the first, the gains always outweigh the losses, while, in the second, they eventually balance out. At present the 'equilibrium' model has the upper hand, but after decades of debate this tricky question has still not been resolved.

BIODIVERSITY

* On the chilly shores of the Antarctic Peninsula there are just two species of flowering plant: a grass, and the Antarctic pearlwort - a plant related to carnations. Eight thousand kilometres (5,000 miles) due north, in the heart of the Amazon rainforest, there are so many flowering plants that the number of species may never be known.

REGIONAL RICHES

* The difference between these two places is summed up in one word: biodiversity. Biodiversity is *a measure of the species richness in any area*, whether it is an individual ecosystem or the whole of the Earth. It is a word that often features in news reports and environmental campaigns, because many biologists believe that biodiversity is linked with ecological stability. Today, global biodiversity is falling fast.

Darwin realized the tropics had more species than anywhere else

WHY THE TROPICS?

✶ During the last century, naturalists like Charles Darwin realized that, in terms of diversity, the tropics far outstrip other regions of the world. Ever since Darwin first stepped ashore in the tropics, over 150 years ago, biologists have debated about why this should be so.

✶ The obvious answer is that the tropics have a favourable climate, which encourages things to grow. With so much energy on the move, there are countless opportunities for new species to exploit. But not all ecologists are convinced that this is the real reason. Another possibility is that the tropics have been good places to live for a very long time – and the longer things live in any area, the more species can evolve.

THE GREAT CRASH

✶ On at least five occasions in the history of life, biodiversity has abruptly crashed. These events – known as mass extinctions – are thought to have been triggered by a variety of factors, including periods of intense volcanic activity, and collisions with objects from outer space. After each mass extinction, species numbers have taken millions of years to return to their original level. Many biologists believe that we are currently living through a sixth mass extinction – this one caused by humans.

KEY WORDS

BIODIVERSITY:
a measure of the number of different kinds of organism within an ecosystem or larger area

volcanic eruptions may have caused some extinctions

PRIVATE - KEEP OFF

Low biodiversity doesn't necessarily mean that life is thin on the ground. In some ecosystems – for example mangrove swamps – the number of species is low, because only a few plants and animals can cope with the local conditions. However, these species have the ecosystem more or less to themselves, and they grow in large numbers.

41

HOW ECOSYSTEMS CHANGE

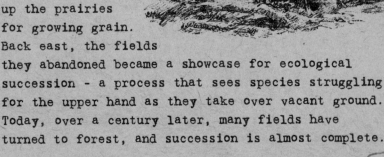

human agricultural practices affect ecosystems

* During the mid-19th century, many American farmers moved westward as improved ploughs opened up the prairies for growing grain. Back east, the fields they abandoned became a showcase for ecological succession - a process that sees species struggling for the upper hand as they take over vacant ground. Today, over a century later, many fields have turned to forest, and succession is almost complete.

Succession in the streets

Every year, humans spend a vast amount of time and effort trying to stop ecological succession taking place. Railway lines are sprayed with herbicides to stop plants springing up among the tracks, and city pavements are swept and repaired to prevent seedlings taking root. If these maintenance operations stopped, plants would eventually clog roads and city centres, producing soil as they die and decompose.

STAGGERED ARRIVÁLS

* In normal circumstances, ecosystems look much the same from one year to the next. Even though individual plants and animals die, the mix of species doesn't seem to change. But, if some kind of disturbance takes place, this equilibrium is upset. Through succession, the land is then reclaimed by nature – often in a predictable way.

* In the eastern USA, the original disturbance took place when farming

keeping plants at bay in the city is a full-time job

fire plays an
important part in
ecological change

first began.
After the farmers
headed west, the
abandoned fields
began to change.
Weeds sprang up in
the place of crops,
often arriving as
wind-borne seeds.
Shrubs took a bit longer to
become established, but they gradually
shaded out the earlier PIONEER SPECIES.
Trees were last to make their presence felt,
but their impact was greatest of all.

PLUS ÇA CHANGE...

✱ The outcome of this slow-motion
contest for space is a more-or-less stable
group of species called a CLIMAX
COMMUNITY. Its precise make-up varies
from place to place. In areas with moist
climates, such as the eastern USA or
western Europe, the climax community is
usually forest. In drier places, such as the
American Midwest or Central Asia,
grassland or scrub forms instead.

✱ *Ecologists once thought of climax*
vegetation as a point at which change more
or less comes to a halt. Today, it is clear
that things are not quite this simple. Even
in a climax community, some species
temporarily get the upper hand, while
others periodically decline. Although
we may not always notice it, change goes
on all the time.

Feeding the flames

In dry places, fire is
one of the
commonest natural
forms of ecological
disturbance. But,
although fire looks
destructive, it is not
always as harmful as it
seems. This is because
some plants have natural
defences against being
burned, while others
actually depend on fires to
survive. The North
American lodgepole pine
(*Pinus contorta*) is a
typical fire-dependent tree.
Its cones open only after
they have been heated by
flames, scattering their
seeds onto the freshly
cleared ground below.

KEY WORDS

SUCCESSION:
an orderly change of the
species in a community,
following any kind of
ecological disturbance

PIONEER SPECIES:
a species that arrives
during the early stage
of succession, but
which is often driven
out by the time
succession is complete

43

only the toughest
species can survive

Up for grabs

In November 1963, a volcanic eruption off the coast of Iceland produced the ultimate in ecological opportunities – a complete new island, waiting to be colonized by living things. Named Surtsey, the island has been the subject of constant research since it first appeared, with all new arrivals being carefully logged. Surtsey's harsh climate means that its plant life is still fairly scant, and consists mainly of mosses, a handful of grasses, and a species of sandwort that spreads by floating seeds. The island is often visited by seabirds, and their droppings provide a natural fertilizer which helps many of the plants to survive.

my droppings provide a natural fertilizer

puffin

STARTING FROM SCRATCH

* Succession isn't always a case of nature reclaiming ground it has recently lost. Sometimes, geological processes create brand-new environments that start out with no inhabitants of their own. Here, succession can be a slow business because, to begin with at least, only the toughest species can survive.

CREATING A BEACH-HEAD

* This kind of natural invasion is called PRIMARY SUCCESSION, in contrast with secondary succession, which takes place in recently inhabited sites. Wherever bare ground is created or newly exposed – for example by volcanic eruptions, receding glaciers or shifting sand – living things get a chance to move in, and primary succession begins.

* Compared with taking over an abandoned field, setting up home on bare ground is no easy matter. Seedlings

there's no soil at all

sometimes manage to germinate in rock crevices, but without soil drought is a constant threat, and getting hold of mineral nutrients can be hard. It is much easier for plants to take root in sand, but the surface can be scorchingly hot, and there is the constant risk of being smothered.

setting up home on bare ground is no easy matter

MAKING GROUND

✱ Where plants do manage to get established, they make it easier for others to follow. As they grow and then die, their remains mix with particles of dust and rock, creating the beginnings of soil. Once a layer of soil has formed, many more plants can follow the early pioneers, throwing the area open to animal life.

✱ In Alaska's Glacier Bay National Park, the ice has retreated over 50km (31 miles) in the last 200 years, allowing ecologists to study this process in detail. Here, frequent rain helps the plants to get established, and, within 25 years of being exposed, the ground already has 5cm (2 inches) of soil and decaying leaves. After 50 years, the soil is 15cm (6 inches) deep, and the ground is covered with small trees. *After 150 years, the trees have formed a forest, and primary succession is complete. In drier climates, succession is often much slower, and soil takes far longer to form.*

THE ULTIMATE PIONEERS

Lichens are often the first living things to colonize bare rock. These slow-growing partnerships between algae and fungi can survive temperatures far below freezing, and droughts many months long. Lichens also produce chemicals that erode rocks, helping to build up soil.

lichens can grow on the barest rocks

THEMES AND VARIATIONS

✱ From a human perspective, there's a world of difference between southern Spain and southern California, or between Borneo and Brazil. But, biologically, these places have lots in common, because their plants and animals have adapted in similar ways. These characteristic groupings are called biomes, and they can be used to map out all life on Earth.

WINE-LOVER'S GUIDE TO BIOMES

Mediterranean scrub – also known as maquis in Europe (and 'chaparral' in the USA) – is one of the smallest and most exclusive of the world's biomes. Apart from the Mediterranean itself, the only other parts of the world where it occurs are California, central Chile, the Cape region of South Africa and Australia. All these parts of the world have long dry summers and mild, moist winters – ideal for growing the biome's most illustrious crop, the grape vine.

LOOKS FAMILIAR

✱ Unlike ecosystems or habitats, individual **biomes can cover large parts of the Earth's surface**. Coniferous forest, for example, reaches three-quarters of the way around the world, from North America, through Scandinavia and across Siberia. The striking thing about this huge swathe of trees is that, from a distance at least, one part of it looks much like any other. Unless you are close enough to identify individual animals and plants, it is very difficult to decide precisely where you are.

✱ This great forest is unusual because it contains few species, and many of them are spread over more than one continent. But all other biomes – including

coniferous forest looks much the same wherever it is

46

deserts, grassland and tundra – share the feature of looking similar wherever they are. They are the great ecological themes of nature – themes that embrace many variations from place to place.

WORKING IN PARALLEL

* Most ecologists recognize about a dozen major biomes. More important than the total number is why recognizable biomes exist at all. The answer is that they have developed through PARALLEL EVOLUTION – a process that creates similar adaptations to similar climatic conditions. Grassland, for example, develops in places where it is too dry for forests to become established, but where there is enough rain to prevent deserts taking their place.

CHANGING THE MAP

* Biomes figure prominently in environmental research, revealing – among other things – how human activity has changed nature's original map of the world. For some biomes, for example coniferous forest, the figures don't look too bad. *For others, the shrinkage has been much more serious. Tropical rainforest, for example, now stands at about half its former extent, while tropical dry forest – down to 30% – has suffered worst of all.* This shrinkage has come about in a variety of ways, and it lies at the heart of most of the ecological problems that face us today.

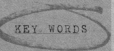

KEY WORDS

BIOME:
the largest kind of ecological grouping within the biosphere, based on characteristic plant formations

the tropical dry forest is disappearing even faster than the rainforest

Underground influence

Climate is the key factor in shaping biomes, but it is not the only one: soil sometimes plays a part. In some parts of the Amazon Basin, the soil is sandy and infertile. Instead of the 'normal' rainforest biome, these areas are covered by *caatinga*, a stunted forest made of spindly trees with leathery leaves.

47

last to
the coast
is a sissy

once squirrels could have
crossed Europe without
leaving the trees

HIGH-RISE HABITATS

* At one time, forest covered about two-fifths of the Earth's land surface. The tree cover was so extensive that if a squirrel chose its route carefully, it could have crossed North America or Europe without ever needing to set foot on the ground. Today, a squirrel trying to repeat this trick would soon run into problems, because forests are much less extensive than they were, and much more fragmented.

LOPSIDED LIFE ZONES

The conifer belt of the far north is the largest forest in the world, covering about 15 million square kilometres (six million square miles). There is no southern equivalent of this forest because there is no land on which it could form. The northern forest is also known as the boreal forest – from Boreas, the mythical Greek god of the north wind.

FORESTS OF THE WORLD

* The type of forest that grows in any area is determined largely by temperature and rainfall. Close to the equator, where the climate is always wet and warm, the result is tropical rainforest. This kind of forest has a wider variety of life than any other terrestrial biome on Earth, but most of it is high up, where it is difficult to see. In the deep shade of the forest floor, animals often seem few and far between.

* Tropical rainforest is rarely out of the headlines, but it is not the only

giant redwood

*it's much easier to fell
a tree than to grow one*

kind of forest in warm regions. Further away from the equator, where there are alternating dry and rainy seasons, rainforest gives way to seasonal forest, and then to dry forest – one of the most threatened forest biomes of all.

SHEDDING LEAVES

✱ In seasonal and dry forests, many trees lose their leaves during the dry season, growing a new set when the rains return. In temperate regions, many broadleaved trees also lose their leaves, but they do it to get through the winter instead of for surviving drought. But farther north, where temperate forest gives way to coniferous forest, the evergreen pattern returns. The trees here have narrow leaves that can survive temperatures far below zero.

INTO THE nTH DIMENSION

✱ Leaves are the main reason why forests are so biologically productive. If the leaf area of a large forest tree is added up, it can easily come to ten times the area of the ground beneath it. When the twigs, branches and trunk are included as well, the total exceeds the ground area many times over. Simply by growing, trees create an elaborate maze of habitats – one that may take several centuries to develop, but which can be felled in a matter of minutes.

Not so hot

Rainforest grows wherever the climate is wet throughout the year. Most of the world's rainforest is in the tropics, but scattered areas are also found in temperate parts of the world, such as the South Island of New Zealand, southern Chile and North America's north-west coast. Many of these temperate rainforests are threatened by logging.

KEY WORDS

BROADLEAVED:
a word used to describe any tree that is a flowering plant, rather than a conifer. Confusingly, some broadleaved trees – such as willows – actually have narrow leaves.

PUT OUT TO GRASS

* Humans evolved in grassland, and it's probably no accident that most people feel more at home in this kind of landscape than they do in woods or forests. In forests, most of the solar energy absorbed goes into building wood and leaves above the ground, but in grasslands up to four-fifths of it ends up underground, where it is used to build roots.

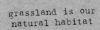

I feel so at home her

grassland is our natural habitat

ON-BOARD ALLIES

Few animals can digest cellulose unaided. Instead, most rely on micro-organisms to do this work for them. RUMINANT mammals, which include cattle, antelopes and their relatives, harbour these micro-organisms in a large stomach chamber called the rumen. Once the micro-organisms have broken down the cellulose, the ruminant can absorb the nutrients that are released.

antelope

HIDDEN STRENGTHS

* Grasses are unusual plants. *Their roots aren't particularly deep, but they can be extraordinarily extensive*. Young rye plants, for example, can have a total root area of over 600 square metres (6,500 square feet) – three times the size of a tennis court. These roots allow grasses to survive difficult times, and they also bind the soil together. In the seasonal droughts that affect natural grasslands, this prevents erosion which would otherwise blow the soil away.

TRICKY FOOD

* Grass leaves contain large amounts of cellulose, a substance that most animals find impossible to digest. However, many

COW

hoofed mammals can survive on grass and little else, thanks to micro-organisms that help them to break it down. Paradoxically, these *mammals actually help grass plants to thrive*, because grasses have adapted to being grazed, whereas other plants die if they are repeatedly nibbled.

MAN-MADE GRASSLANDS

✳ Natural grassland originally covered about a third of the Earth's land surface. Most of it has been transformed by farming, but people have also created new grasslands through deforestation. The interplay between people and grassland has been a complex one, but the result today is that natural grassland has shrunk to about a quarter of its original extent.

✳ In some places, forests were converted to grassland so long ago that it's difficult to tell whether it is natural or not. But without sheep, cattle and other domesticated grazers, ecological succession (pp. 42-43) would begin, and this 'anthropogenic' grassland would eventually revert to forest once more.

I'm off to scatter a few tree seeds

KEY WORDS

RUMINANT:
a hoofed plant-eating mammal with a complex digestive system. While they are not feeding, ruminants 'chew the cud' – meaning that they regurgitate partly digested food and chew it a second time.
ANTHROPOGENIC:
in ecology, an environmental effect caused by humans

Grass versus trees

Savanna is tropical grassland with a scattering of trees. In this kind of environment the balance between trees and grass is always changing, with animals and fires helping to nudge it in one direction or the other. Elephants, for example, destroy trees and encourage grass, but they also spread tree seeds, scattering them in their dung.

elephants spread seeds in their dung

51

DRY LIFE

* While forests and grasslands have been transformed by human activities, until now the world's deserts have emerged largely unscathed. Uniquely among the world's biomes, they enjoy the distinction of expanding as a result of human impact - something that creates problems where they encroach on land used for growing food.

deserts are the driest
places on earth

OUTLOOK: DRY

True deserts generally have less than 15cm (6 inches) of rain a year. A semidesert is somewhere that has between 15 and 30cm (6 and 12 inches). Together, they cover about a quarter of the earth's land surface.

Lasting impressions

Because desert plants grow very slowly, it takes a long time for them to recover from any damage. In the late 1970s, tank tracks were still visible in the desert of southern Tunisia, 35 years after the battles of the Second World War.

SURVIVAL STRATEGIES

* Deserts are places where water evaporates much faster than it is replaced. Although most of them are hot by day, their daily temperature range is greater than in any other biome, with the mercury sometimes falling below freezing after dark. Most of the world's deserts are in the subtropics, but desert conditions are also found at much higher latitudes: desert valleys exist even in Antarctica.

* In deserts, living things have two main methods of survival: they either tough it out, or they skip the bad times

prickly pear cactu

altogether. Cacti are supreme exponents of the 'tough it out' approach. They have extensive roots which spread out close to the ground surface so that they can quickly intercept the water that falls during sporadic storms. Having got hold of this water, they make sure that very little of it goes to waste. Cacti are slow-growing but often very long-lived.

Opuntia microdasys cactus

✱ Desert plants called 'ephemerals' are exactly the opposite. They germinate within hours of rain, and then put all their energy into a break-neck dash to flower. *Once they have produced and scattered their seeds, they wither and die.*

DESERTS ON THE MOVE

✱ Most of the world's deserts are created by zones of high-pressure air that circle the Earth. This air contains little moisture, so it very rarely rains. Deserts also form in the centre of continents, and in 'rain shadows' in the lee of high mountains. Patagonia, for example, is kept arid by the Andes, which block rain-bearing winds from the west. But like man-made grasslands, deserts can also be created by people. This happens when dry ground is stripped of its plants, often by overgrazing, allowing the wind to blow away the soil. This process – called DESERTIFICATION – is now a major problem in many parts of the world.

where's the water?

KEY WORDS

EPHEMERAL:
in botany, a plant that completes its life cycle in a very short time

WATER-WORN LANDSCAPES

Because they have so little vegetation, deserts are easily eroded by water that falls in intermittent storms. The lack of plants and soil means that most of this water runs off in flash floods, instead of sinking into the ground.

you've got to be tough to live up here

THE BIG CHILL

* At high altitudes and high latitudes, living things face severe problems simply staying alive. Among them are sub-zero temperatures, high winds and frequent lack of food. But life in mountains and near the poles has some advantages. With few species competing for a share of the action, it is easier to be a success.

Heads down!

In tundra, high winds force plants to adopt a ground-hugging way of life. In the winter, these ground huggers become covered by snow, which protects them from severe temperatures outside. For tundra plants, survival is hardest in places where the snow cover is very light.

IT'S SO BRACING

* In most parts of the world, average air temperatures drop by about 6.5°C for every 1,000m climbed (3.5°F per 1,000ft). Known as the TEMPERATURE LAPSE RATE, this explains the ecological similarities between places that are high up, and ones that are closer to the poles. For example, in Canada's Northwest Territories, the ground is covered in Arctic tundra – a treeless expanse of grasses and cushion-shaped plants growing among snowfields and frost-shattered rock. About 3,000km (1,850 miles) farther south, an almost identical environment called alpine tundra can be seen on the peaks of the Rocky Mountains. The difference between the two is that the Canadian tundra is close to sea level, while the Rocky Mountain tundra is 3,500m (11,500ft) up.

LIFE AROUND THE CLOCK

* As biomes go, tundra is a place of extremes. This is particularly true of Arctic tundra, because seasonal changes here include not only variations in temperature, but also in day-length. The 24-hour daylight of the brief Arctic summer creates one of the most concentrated bursts of biological activity seen anywhere on the planet, as plants bloom, nestlings hatch, and billions of aphids and mosquitoes emerge to breed.

mosquito

* Round-the-clock daylight also helps to explain why marine life is so abundant near the poles. Photosynthetic plankton populations drop to rock-bottom levels in the winter, but in the spring and summer they boom, generating an immense supply of food that is passed on through fish, birds and mammals.

* Icy sea water may not seem like an ideal backdrop for living things, but, surprisingly, in some ways its coldness is actually an advantage. This is because cold sea water can hold far more dissolved oxygen and carbon dioxide than warm sea water, helping marine life to thrive.

COME IN, THE WATER'S LOVELY!

In the depths of winter, air temperatures in the **Arctic and Antarctic can drop below -40°C** (-40°F), but sea water temperatures never fall below -1.8°C (28.8°F), because, below this point, salt water freezes. As a result, it's far warmer in the water than out. The downside is that sea water is much better than air at conducting heat, so it can quickly drain warmth from animal bodies. Polar birds and mammals protect themselves against this heat loss with a layer of insulating fat, or blubber.

fur and fat keep polar bears warm

come on, it's warm

FRESHWATER WORLDS

* Ecologists sometimes seem obsessively interested in freshwater environments, but with a little first-hand experience it's easy to see why. These environments often teem with life. Unfortunately, they are also often first in the firing line when pollution causes environmental change.

it's crystal clear

mountain streams don't carry any nutrients to support life

STRATIFIED WORLD

Because the density of water varies with its temperature, deep lakes are often partitioned into two layers, each with its own distinctive life. The layers are separated by an invisible boundary called a <u>THERMOCLINE</u>. This partitioning is most marked in summer, when the surface is warmest. In autumn, the thermocline often breaks down as the surface water cools and sinks, mixing up the layers that were previously separate.

FEEDING FRENZY

* Nothing can survive in pure fresh water because all forms of water life need some basic mineral nutrients. In mountain streams and lakes, the surrounding soil is often infertile – which means that the supply of nutrients is poor. As a result, the water contains few plants and animals, and is often crystal clear.

* These <u>OLIGOTROPHIC</u> conditions contrast with the <u>EUTROPHIC</u> conditions that are common on lower ground. Here, ponds and lakes are surrounded by fertile land, so nutrients are rarely in short supply. Rainwater washes them in from the soil, and spring often brings a population explosion of microscopic life. This boom of biological productivity generates lots of food for animals, and produces a steady rain of organic leftovers that form a rich mud on the lake bed.

✱ However, it is possible to have too much of a good thing. When nutrient-rich synthetic fertilizers are washed into streams and rivers, the population explosion can get out of hand. Instead of sustaining life, it can end with a sudden collapse.

DISAPPEARING WETLANDS

✱ Over long periods of time – usually hundreds or thousands of years – shallow water is often invaded by plants. This slow and stealthy form of <u>ECOLOGICAL SUCCESSION</u> creates wetlands, where vegetation covers the waterlogged ground. Wetland soil is deep and rich, because plant remains often accumulate faster than they break down.

✱ Altogether, wetlands cover only a small fraction of the earth's surface, but their biological importance is out of all proportion to their size. They act as natural water-filtering systems and erosion barriers, and as homes and wintering grounds for huge numbers of birds. But over the last two centuries, the world's wetlands have been disappearing fast, with many being drained and turned into fields. In the USA alone, about 200,000 hectares (500,000 acres) are being destroyed every year.

> ## KEY WORDS
>
> **EUTROPHIC:** literally 'healthy nourishment'; applied to water that is enriched by the nutrients needed by plants and phytoplankton for growth
>
> **OLIGOTROPHIC:** literally 'little nourishment'; applied to water that contains relatively low concentrations of nutrients

pond life

COASTS AND SEAS

coastlines are affected by human activity

✶ Physically and biologically, coasts and seas are as different as chalk and cheese. Coasts change with each ebb and flow of the tide, but the open sea is a place where conditions are much more static, and sudden change extremely rare. Of all the environments on Earth, the sea has been the last one to feel the impact of mankind.

Squatters and movers

Marine biologists categorize living things according to where they live, and also how they move. LITTORAL species live on the shore, while PELAGIC species live in the open water and BENTHIC species live in or on the seabed. PLANKTONIC life-forms drift with the currents, while NEKTONIC organisms are big enough to swim through the water.

PLUMBING THE DEPTHS

✶ Ecologists have amassed plenty of data about coasts and their natural inhabitants – particularly those that don't swim away – but less is known about life in the open sea. Salinity, temperature and oxygen levels all have an effect on what lives where, but a much more important factor is light.

✶ Even in the *clearest sea water, which is found off Antarctica*, light penetrates no more than about 300m (1,000ft). Above this level, in the PHOTIC ZONE, photosynthetic organisms can generate food. Below it, in the perpetually dark APHOTIC ZONE, photosynthesis does not work, so such organisms cannot survive. As a result, life below the light barrier depends almost entirely on whatever drifts down from above. These organic titbits include a steady blizzard of dead micro-organisms, together with occasional but much more substantial fare, such as dead fish, seabirds, seals and even whales. As the average depth of the oceans is over 3,500m (11,500ft), the photic zone is a tiny fraction of the oceans as a whole.

I think I've found a shoal

sonar operator

FOOD FROM THE SEA

✱ For thousands of years, people have exploited coasts for food. Some idea of the haul is provided by the shell mounds of North America, left behind by Native Americans who collected molluscs along the shore. Fishing is also an ancient activity, although not on anything like the scale seen today.

fishing trawler

✱ Unlike land habitats, the sea hasn't been transformed by human occupation, but it has been increasingly affected by the way we live. Most of these changes have been concentrated close to the coast, in coral reefs and in the shallow water over continental shelves. *In some fishing grounds in the North Atlantic, the seabed is criss-crossed with tracks gouged out by trawler nets, showing that even this distant world is now within easy reach.*

FALSE BOTTOMS

The invention of sonar in 1917 made it possible to chart the seabed using sound. But when oceanographers started to use this new technology they were startled to find previously uncharted 'shallows' in deep, open water. *Officially labelled 'deep scattering layers', they turned out to be shoals of fish and animal plankton.* These shoals carry out daily vertical migrations, feeding near the surface at night, and hiding in deeper water during daylight hours.

59

THE GEOGRAPHY OF LIFE

* If climate was the main factor determining what lives where, penguins would live in the Arctic and yaks would roam the Rocky Mountains. But, in the real world, nature doesn't work this way. The reason why not is that living things come with a history - one that ties them to a particular habitat in a specific part of the world.

OK let's go live in the Arctic then

HISTORY TIME

* Every species on Earth originates just once. Some never get far from where they first appear, while others manage to spread much farther. However, no matter how good a plant or animal is at spreading, it will eventually come up against geographical or climatic barriers that it is unable to cross. *As a result, its distribution is restricted.*

MAPPING IT OUT

The science of biogeography was pioneered by the English naturalist **Alfred Russel Wallace** (1823–1913). Famous for his work on evolution (he almost pipped Charles Darwin to the post), Wallace travelled throughout the tropics and spent many years in Southeast Asia. He recognized that the world can be divided up into six 'faunal regions'. These are the NEARCTIC (North America), NEOTROPICAL (Central and South America), PALEARCTIC (Europe, North Africa, central and northern Asia), ETHIOPIAN (Africa and Arabia), ORIENTAL (southern Asia) and AUSTRALASIAN (Australia, New Zealand and New Guinea). Each region has its own characteristic animal life.

Alfred Wallace

* Life's regional flavour works on a huge variety of scales. In the Hawaiian Islands, for example, many species of snail are confined to individual valleys, while, in tropical Africa, many freshwater fish live only in particular lakes. On a much broader level, whole groups of species tend to be restricted to major chunks of the Earth's surface, known as biogeographic regions.

HOME ALONE

* *These regions have come about largely because the continents are on the move. For millions of years they have repeatedly collided and separated again, carrying their plant and animal life with them.* Continents that have been joined together relatively recently – such as North America and Europe – tend to have similar wildlife because their species have had a chance to mix. Landmasses that have been isolated for a long time, such as Australia and Madagascar, have a high proportion of ENDEMIC SPECIES – ones that are found nowhere else in the world.

* Endemic plants and animals are highly vulnerable to species introduced from outside, because they often lack what it takes to compete. For a remote island like Mauritius, the impact of these introduced species has been profound. Mauritius lost its most famous inhabitant, the dodo, in about 1680, and today nearly 40% of its native bird and mammal species are in danger of becoming extinct.

Alfred Wegener

You cannot be serious!

The theory of continental drift was first proposed in 1912 by the German geologist **Alfred Wegener** (1880–1930). It was widely derided at the time, but in the 1960s evidence of sea-floor spreading showed that it is true.

ONLY HOME

The tiny Devil's Hole pupfish is believed to have one of the most restricted distributions of any animal on Earth. The entire species – about 400 strong – lives in a single pool in the Nevada Desert.

Dodo

61

DISTANT RELATIONS

* Like slow-moving dodgems at a fairground, the continents have charted a complex course during their millions of years adrift. At the same time, sea levels have risen and fallen, and the Earth's climate has warmed and cooled. These geological and climatic changes have all affected living things, sometimes keeping close relatives together, at other times forcing them apart.

HOPPING ACROSS

Southwest Ireland is an unlikely home for a remarkable plant: the strawberry tree *(Arbutus unedo)*. Today, most strawberry trees grow around the sun-baked shores of the Mediterranean, but at the end of the last Ice Age they managed to spread up the west coast of Europe, reaching Ireland via a land-bridge. The land-bridge then disappeared, leaving a pocket of strawberry trees stranded in their Irish outpost.

PARTING COMPANY

* The plant and animal kingdoms both contain groups of species that are closely related, but which live in widely separated parts of the world. For example, tapirs are found in Central and South America, and also in Southeast Asia. Magnolias grow in North America and also in China, while southern beeches grow in Chile and New Zealand – two countries with similar climates, but thousands of miles apart. These <u>DISJUNCTIVE DISTRIBUTIONS</u> puzzled 19th-century naturalists, who came up with a number of ingenious explanations for their existence. However, they missed the true reason – that continents can split and separate, dividing plants or animals that once lived side by side.

SINKING BRIDGES

✱ Continental drift explains giant gaps in species distribution – the kind that can span the whole of the Earth. But separation can also occur when the climate is changing fast, altering local conditions or the layout of the land.

✱ When the average temperature is dropping, sea levels fall because the size of the Earth's ice-caps increases. Low sea levels expose shallow parts of the seabed, allowing plants and animals to spread to offshore islands. But, when the temperature starts to rise again, the effect is reversed. The land-bridges are flooded, stranding anything that cannot fly or swim.

✱ Rising temperatures can also force cold-adapted species uphill, stranding them on high ground. This has happened to a tree called the Spanish fir, which retreated uphill at the end of the last Ice Age, becoming 'trapped' in the mountains of southern Spain. If GLOBAL WARMING produces another steep temperature rise, many other plants and animals may find themselves climbing higher to escape the heat.

The mysterious magpie

The azure-winged magpie (*Cyanopica cyana*) has one of the most bizarre distributions in the animal world. It is found in the Far East, and also in Portugal and Spain. One explanation for the huge gap in its range is that it was brought to Europe by traders several centuries ago. Another – considered more likely by many ornithologists – is that it once lived across the whole of Europe and Asia, but was forced to retreat eastwards and westwards by climate change. Eventually, this left no magpies in the middle.

species can be separated by rising water levels

63

CHAPTER 2

A QUESTION OF NUMBERS

✱ Whether you are a lemming, a lichen on a rock, or one of the Earth's six billion human beings, there are three certainties in life: you are born, you get older, and sooner or later you die. Putting numbers to these events - and others as well - helps to explain why the Earth isn't buried under mounds of fish or bacteria, and why populations rise and fall.

there are three certainties in life - you are born, you live and then you die

I'm really happy being a lemming

Are you one, or a group?

For ecological number-crunchers, plants can be harder to deal with than animals. One of the reasons for this is that individuals aren't always clear-cut. Clumps of aspen or bracken, for example, are often connected by underground stems or roots, making it difficult to decide how many 'individuals' the clump contains.

STICKING TOGETHER

✱ The most important figures in ecology are ones that relate to populations. Used in its biological sense, a population is a COLLECTION OF INDIVIDUALS THAT BELONG TO THE SAME SPECIES, and which live in the same area at the same time. For example, the endangered whooping cranes that breed in Alberta's Wood Buffalo National Park make up a single (and sadly depleted) population. On the other hand, the puffins that breed on coasts in the North Atlantic make up a large number of populations because, to varying degrees, each group is separated from its neighbours.

crane

WE HAVE LIFT-OFF

✱ A key feature of populations is that there is free gene flow within them – in other words, there are no environmental barriers to prevent any pair of adults getting together to breed. Another key characteristic is that, given the opportunity, their numbers have the potential to increase. In some populations, such as a herd of elephants, the rate of increase is fairly low, but in small animals and most

members of populations can breed together

plants it is so huge that the numbers of offspring involved quickly become mind-boggling. Herring, for example, could theoretically fill the entire Atlantic within a few years. Smaller organisms, such as bacteria, have even higher reproductive rates, so they could theoretically swamp the Earth in a matter of weeks.

✱ *Fortunately, this doesn't happen. Instead, population numbers in nature often remain surprisingly similar from year to year. It's a fact that makes our own population boom all the more remarkable.*

TAKING A CENSUS

Working out the sizes of natural populations isn't always as straightforward as it sounds. With animals, a useful short-cut is the mark/recapture technique. First, a number of individuals are caught and identified, often by marking them with a tag or spot of paint. These animals are then released, and several days later another batch is caught. In this second batch, the relative proportion of marked to unmarked animals is used to work out an estimate of the total size of the population.

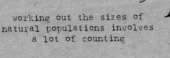

working out the sizes of natural populations involves a lot of counting

65

How long can you last?

Charts called life tables give a full analysis of the age structure of a population. They show, among other things, mortality rates and further expectation of life, both of which change with age. These tables have been worked out in great detail for human populations, and life insurance companies use them to calculate what size of premium their clients should pay.

A CERTAIN AGE

* For most living things, life is a precarious business. But, looked at statistically, some periods of life are much more dangerous than others. Young sparrows, for example, are ten times more likely to die in their first year than in their second, but, after that, their chances of surviva. improve. For wild populations - and anyone buying life insurance - these age-linked differences have important implications.

I can sell you a great policy

insurers take a bet on your chances of dying

UNFAIR SHARES

Life pyramids are often split into two halves, showing the relative numbers of males and females at each age. In humans, age pyramids are slightly unequal at their base, because more boys are born than girls. They also become lopsided towards the top, because more women than men survive into old age.

BIRTHDAY BLUES

* Some species of plants and animals have completely separate generations, so that each one breeds and dies before the next one begins. But, in most living things, populations are made up of OVERLAPPING GENERATIONS, with a range of ages mixed together. Charts called AGE PYRAMIDS show how many individuals are present at each particular age.

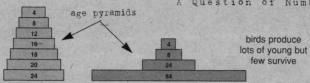

mammals produce few young, but most survive

birds produce lots of young but few survive

age pyramids for mammals and birds

★ These pyramids tell some interesting stories. In the case of sparrows, for example, the pyramid has a very broad base, showing that sparrow populations include a large number of first-year young. But at the next layer, corresponding to Year 2, the pyramid suddenly contracts, because over 90% of the young birds have died. From here upwards, the pyramid gradually tapers to a point, showing that, once a sparrow has reached its first birthday, it runs roughly the same risk of dying each year.

MIDDLE-AGE SPREAD

★ *The shape of age pyramids varies between different species.* In sea fish, for example, age pyramids are often massively bottom-heavy, because vast numbers of young fish die within weeks of hatching from their eggs. In whales and other slow-breeding mammals, age pyramids are taller and much narrower, because a large proportion of young survive into old age.

★ *Age pyramids also vary within species, in different populations and at different times.* If reproductive rates suddenly increase, the bottom of the pyramid bulges outwards as a wave of young start to head up the pyramid towards reproductive age. When this happens, a POPULATION BOOM is under way.

KEY WORDS

LIFE EXPECTANCY: the average length of time for which an individual or group can expect to live

MORTALITY: the probability of dying within a set period of time

grey squirrel

On the up

Because many living things die when they are young, life expectancy doesn't decline at a steady rate: instead, it often increases during the first few years. For example, grey squirrels have a life expectancy of about 1.01 years shortly after birth, but 1.9 years between the ages of two and three.

67

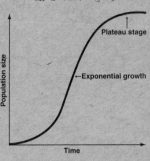

an S-curve graph

Plateau stage

Population size

←Exponential growth

Time

THE S-CURVE

* With human numbers increasing at a record rate, the way populations grow is one of the hottest topics in environmental science. Studies of animals can't be related directly to the human world, but they do show what happens during natural population booms, and - more revealing still - what eventually brings these booms to a halt.

Cashing in

Population growth is very much like compound interest, and it can be calculated in the same way. *For example, if you invest $1,000 for ten years at an interest rate of 5%, the amount you will eventually get back – assuming the bank doesn't go bust – is worked out by the formula $x(1+i)^n$.* In this formula, x is the initial amount you have invested, i is the rate of interest, and n is the number of years. The answer comes out at $1,629. This is also the number of animals that would be produced after ten years by a population that grows at a rate of 5%.

overpopulation can be a serious problem

BEETLEMANIA

* *In the lab, insects are often used for studying the way populations change.* Some beetles can survive on nothing but flour, making it easy to raise closed populations and to monitor the way they rise and fall. When a typical flour beetle colony is set up, its numbers initially increase fairly slowly. The rate of increase then starts to accelerate until it reaches a maximum figure. After a period of rapid growth, it then starts to drop back, until growth finally comes to a halt.

✱ Shown as a graph, this kind of growth produces an S-shaped curve. The beginning of the slope marks a period of exponential growth, which is a time when the rate of increase is itself increasing. The maximum steepness of the slope is determined by the beetles' REPRODUCTIVE POTENTIAL, which is itself fixed by the time they need to complete their life-cycles, and the number of eggs they can produce. The faster the beetles turn out eggs, the steeper the slope becomes.

flour beetles make good guinea pigs for population study

DOUBLING UP

✱ An easy way to interpret this slope is to turn it into a doubling time. As a population's growth rate goes up, its doubling time goes down, reaching a minimum when its members are reproducing for all they are worth. *For flour beetles, the minimum doubling time is roughly ten days.* For field voles it is about two-and-a-half months, while for large mammals it is often over ten years.

✱ These figures don't mean that animal populations actually grow at these rates. What they do show is just how rapidly species are capable of expanding when nothing stands in their way.

KEY WORDS

EXPONENTIAL GROWTH:
a rate of growth that is affected by the size of the population that is doing the growing. The larger the population, the faster the rate of growth.

REPRODUCTIVE POTENTIAL:
the rate at which a population grows in ideal conditions. Also known as **biotic potential**.

field vole

69

HITTING THE BRAKES

* In nature, populations hit their maximum possible growth rates only when conditions are ideal. But, even on the rare occasions when this

you're treading on my toes

humans are reproducing at a record rate

happens, the good times cannot last forever. Sooner or later, environmental factors start to slow things down, and the more crowded a population gets, the more important some of them become.

FOR THE GREATER GOOD

In some circumstances, animals do seem to behave in ways that benefit others rather than themselves. For example, parent birds – particularly jays – are sometimes helped by other adults that have no young of their own. In most cases, the helpers turn out to be close relatives of the parents, and therefore of their young. By lending a hand at the nest, they ensure that the young survive and pass on their jointly-held genes.

TOO GOOD TO LAST

* The factors that damp down population growth work in two different ways. Physical factors, such as bad weather, usually have more or less the same effect regardless of how big a population becomes. Biological factors work in a subtler way, because they are directly linked to population density: the higher this becomes, the greater effect they have. These factors include *the increased risks of disease and attack that often come with higher numbers*, and – most importantly of all – *growing competition for the resources that are essential for life.*

* Ecologists have long debated which of these factors is more important in keeping population size under control. The

jay

there's just not enough room for both of us

consensus today is that both play their part, although at particular times one may be much more important than another.

PROFUSION VERSUS PRUDENCE

✷ The maximum number of individuals that an area can support indefinitely is called the area's CARRYING CAPACITY. In natural environments, populations usually wobble about just below the carrying capacity. Sometimes they overshoot it, but sooner or later, numbers drop back to a sustainable level.

✷ The narrowness of these wobbles has made some ecologists wonder if animals have ways of keeping their numbers under control – for example by 'deliberately' reducing their family sizes when food is in short supply. It sounds an admirable idea, but most experts now think it is unlikely.

Self-regulation would require natural selection to work in an unusual way, favouring 'prudent' populations and ignoring the interests of individuals. It is more likely that self-interest – rather than prudence – helps animals to survive hard times.

pressure on resources is one result of overpopulation

CARRYING CAPACITY: the maximum population size that an environment can sustain on a long-term basis

Gloom and doom

One of the first people to write about the biological factors influencing population growth was the English clergyman and economist **Thomas Malthus** (1766–1834). In his *Essay on the Principle of Population* he pointed out the disparity between the exponential increase in the human population and the linear increase in the food supply. Malthus concluded that the human population would always rise until it was held in check by famine, disease and war. In 1838, **Charles Darwin** realized that Malthus' ideas could be applied to the natural world – a breakthrough that helped him to formulate his theory of evolution.

WINNER TAKES ALL

* Competition with next-door neighbours is only one side of the struggle for survival. As well as vying with their own kind, living things also have to compete with members of other species. Some classic ecological experiments, dating from the 1930s, show that the more similar the competitors are, the more intense this struggle becomes.

come on, theirs was finished last week

there are many aspects to the struggle for survival

Turning the tables

Research carried out in the 1950s by the American ecologist **Thomas Park** showed that, when two species compete, the outcome often depends on environmental conditions. Park found that when flour beetles are raised in cool dry conditions, a species called *Tribolium confusum* nearly always outstrips its close relative *Tribolium castaneum*. But, when Park adjusted the beetles' 'climate', making it moister, the tables were turned and *Tribolium castaneum* came out on top.

THE DEADLY DUET

* The experiments were carried out by the Russian biologist **G. F. Gause**, who worked with freshwater micro-organisms called *Paramecium*. Gause took two very similar species – *Paramecium aurelia* and *Paramecium caudatum* – and raised them in laboratory flasks, both together and on their own. Once these miniature environments had been stocked with food, he monitored the numbers of each species as time went by.

✱ On their own, both species showed typical S-shaped growth curves, with their numbers eventually levelling out. But, when they were raised together, the outcome was very different – disastrously so as far as *Paramecium caudatum* was concerned. Within two weeks, its numbers crashed to almost zero, while *Paramecium aurelia* flourished.

AVOIDING THE CHALLENGE

✱ Experiments like this highlight a harsh fact of life: when two species compete directly, there is no such thing as fair shares for all. The species with the competitive edge presses home its advantage until the other is muscled out. This is known as Gause's principle, or the PRINCIPLE OF COMPETITIVE EXCLUSION

✱ At first glance, this winner-takes-all scenario seems to be bad news for *Paramecium caudatum* and its kind. However, things are not quite as bad as they seem. In the real world, conditions rarely stay constant for long and, when they change the current winner may lose the upper hand. *Furthermore, species don't take competition lying down. Instead, they adapt to it, subtly altering the way they live.* The result of this process is that every species develops its own ecological niche (pages 36–7), and, no matter how similar two species appear, they rarely compete head-on.

SQUIRREL WARS

When two previously isolated species are brought into contact, competition can have dramatic effects. An example of this occurred when American grey squirrels were introduced into England and Wales between the 1870s and 1930s. Grey squirrels proved to have a strong competitive edge over Britain's native red squirrels, and they forced the red squirrels from most of their former range. A similar furry take-over took place in Italy's Po Valley when grey squirrels were released there in 1948.

red squirrel

grey squirrel

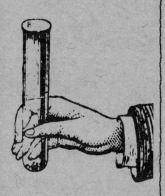

no, wait! I promise
something will happen
in a minute!

YOUR NUMBER'S UP

During the mid-1920s, the American mathematician **Alfred Lotka** and the Italian biologist **Vittora Volterra** independently came up with mathematical equations that predicted what happens when species compete for the same resources, and when predators feed on their prey. Now known as the Lotka-Volterra equations, they provide a theoretical basis for the outcomes that Gause produced with his test-tube experiments.

PREDATORS AND PREY

✱ G. F. Gause's experiments also explored the most deadly form of competition - when one species hunts down and kills another. Using a microscopic but rapacious hunter called *Didinium*, he found that there are a number of long-term outcomes when predators are released on their prey.

NO HIDING PLACE

I don't war
to be the pr
any more!

✱ Like *Paramecium*, *Didinium* consists of a single cell. Although it is only about 0.1mm (0.004 inches) long, it has a giant appetite, consuming up to a dozen *Paramecium* a day. *This speedy rate of food intake makes it an ideal species for studying predation, because it has a rapid impact on the numbers of its prey.*

✱ When Gause unleashed this microscopic hunter, he discovered that its population, and that of its prey, generally behaved in one of three ways. If he kept the 'environment' as simple as it could possibly be – a plain test-tube filled with water – the predators quickly tracked down their luckless victims. When they had eaten them all, they promptly died out. But when he made the environment slightly more complex, by adding some glass wool at the bottom of the test-tube, the prospects for the prey improved dramatically. In the microscopic game of hide-and-seek that followed, some *Paramecium* always managed to escape attack. *But once the predators had eaten all the food out in the open, they quickly starved to death.*

THE THIRD WAY

✳ In real life, hunters and their prey are not shut away in sealed environments. Animals come and go, abandoning areas where food is short and moving to places where there is more on offer. To mimic this situation, *Gause periodically added small numbers of predators or prey to the mix, and then charted the results.* This time, neither species died out. Instead, the two populations started to oscillate, with the predators following the ups and downs of their prey. Each time the prey numbers began to fall, the predators also dropped, giving the prey a chance to recover. Once that recovery set in, the predators had more to eat, and the cycle began again.

✳ Unlike the previous experiments, this one created a world in which THE TWO SPECIES COULD COEXIST. Despite its simplicity, it reflects what often happens in nature itself.

hunting is the deadliest form of competition

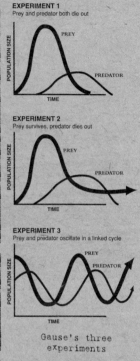

EXPERIMENT 1
Prey and predator both die out

POPULATION SIZE

PREY

PREDATOR

TIME

EXPERIMENT 2
Prey survives, predator dies out

POPULATION SIZE

PREY

PREDATOR

TIME

EXPERIMENT 3
Prey and predator oscillate in a linked cycle

POPULATION SIZE

PREY

PREDATOR

TIME

Gause's three experiments

Changing tactics

One of the problems in predicting the balance between predators and prey is that a predator's behaviour can change. *For example, when a prey species is rare, a potential predator may not bother to pursue it, but when it is more common, the same predator may include it in its diet.* This kind of change, called a 'FUNCTIONAL RESPONSE', gives rare prey species a better chance of survival.

BOOM AND BUST

* In 1845, the Hudson's Bay Company began to keep accurate records of the number of animal pelts being purchased from trappers in northern Canada. A century later, ecologists realized that these records provided unique evidence about the way one particular predator affects its prey. However, interpreting the data turned out to be not quite as straightforward as it seemed.

this is lynx not minx

Staying in synch

The rise and fall of snowshoe hares and lynxes was first analysed by the pioneering British ecologist **Charles Elton** (1900–91) in 1924. In research published in the 1940s, Elton showed that Arctic foxes also have a ten-year cycle over most of their range, but where they feed on lemmings they have a four-year cycle instead.

Canadian lynx

THE TEN-YEAR CYCLE

* The predator in question was the Canadian lynx, and its prey was the snowshoe hare. Both animals were hunted for their fur, so the company records supplied reliable data about the numbers of both species. The figures were striking: *hare numbers boomed and then crashed on a ten-year cycle*, with lynx numbers following suit. For fur trappers, it was usually a case of two or three really good years followed by seven or eight much leaner ones.

* On the face of it, this kind of PERIODIC CYCLING looks exactly like

we're off to find food

the results Gause obtained with his test-tube experiments, albeit on a much larger scale. And, initially at least, this is precisely the way the records were interpreted. But then something spoiled the show. On Anticosti Island in the Gulf of St Lawrence, ecologists discovered hares that were living without lynxes, wolves or any other large predators – and their numbers went up and down on a ten-year cycle as well.

WHO CONTROLS WHO?

✱ This discovery prompted some rethinking. Further research revealed that the key factor affecting the snowshoe hare population was not attack by predators, but the AVAILABILITY OF FOOD. During the long northern winters, snowshoe hares feed mainly on aspen twigs. When hares are thin on the ground, the aspens soon recover, but if there are lots of hares, the winter food supply begins to run out. *Large numbers of hares perish before the spring,* and their numbers do not rally until the aspens have had time to recover – and that takes several years.

✱ The moral of this tale is that nature is much more complex than a test tube. Instead of controlling their prey, some predators are helpless followers in the numbers game.

where have all the aspens gone?

TIME TO GET OUT

Steep oscillations in population size are a characteristic feature of species that live in simple environments, such as the northern tundra. The most famous of these species is the lemming, which has three- or four-year cycles. At the peak of each cycle, lemming numbers can increase by up to a thousandfold. Overcrowding or shortage of food (biologists are not sure which) then drives them to abandon their normal home range. Despite stories of mass suicides, lemmings don't show any eagerness to jump off cliffs: most migrating lemmings are eaten by predators, or die of hunger.

teamwork is
the key to
everything

Worlds within worlds

Wood-eating termites digest wood with the help of micro-organisms that live in their digestive systems – a similar arrangement to that which allows cows to digest grass. At one time it was thought that these micro-organisms produced the enzymes needed to break down wood, but things have turned out to be more complicated than that. The micro-organisms themselves contain their own symbiotic partners – in this case bacteria – and it is these that secrete the digestive enzymes. Stranger still, the micro-organisms move through the termite's gut with the help of other bacteria, which are attached to their outer surface. These bacteria beat like oars, pushing their partners along.

LIVING TOGETHER

* When two species interact, the options are not limited just to competing or playing predators and prey. Sometimes one species stands to gain by sticking close to another, or alternatively both may benefit by forming a working team. Partnerships like these are examples of symbiosis - convenient arrangements that crop up in many walks of life.

we'll do better in partnershi

sometimes it's better to work with another species instead of competing

JOINING FORCES

* The teamwork form of symbiosis is the most common in the natural world. It's known as MUTUALISM, because it provides a mutual benefit for both of the partners involved. Many people – including ecologists – use symbiosis to mean mutualism, but, strictly speaking, symbiosis covers other ways of life as well.

* Mutualism is so widespread throughout the natural world that most living things depend on it either directly or indirectly for survival. Many of the plants we eat reproduce thanks to the work of insects that spread their pollen. Most of the trees that we use for timber grow with the help of fungi which live in or on their roots, helping them to extract nutrients from the soil. All the grazing mammals that provide meat and milk do so with the help of micro-organisms. Without them, they would not be able to digest their food (see pages 50–51).

ALLIES IN DISGUISE

* In some cases, mutualism involves more than 'scratch-my-back-and-I'll-scratch-yours'. For example, the fungi that grow in and around plant roots reproduce by forming microscopic spores. These spores are often spread through the faeces of small mammals such as voles, which use the fungi's fruiting bodies as food. The plants, fungi and voles form an interlocking trio, with each species benefiting from the others' presence.

* *Interactions like these increase the complexity of ecosystems, and they make it unwise to condemn species for 'causing harm'. Often, species that are thought of as pests – particularly insects – are absolutely essential for an ecosystem's health.*

KEY WORDS

MUTUALISM:
a relationship between two different species in which both partners benefit

SYMBIOSIS:
a partnership between two different species, often (but not necessarily) to their mutual advantage. Some ecologists restrict the term symbiosis to partnerships in which the participants are closely physically linked. In **endosymbiosis**, one partner lives inside the other.

thank goodness for my micro-organisms

cows have micro-organisms in their gut to help them digest grass

EXTINCTION

* Extinction, like death, is an inescapable fact of life. Since life first began, over 3.5 billion years ago, it has swept away over 99% of all the species that have ever existed. So, if it happens all the time, why should it be a subject for concern? The answer is that - thanks to human beings - it is taking place at an ever-increasing rate.

meteor strikes are one cause of extinctions

THE LIVING DEAD

One of the grim realities of extinction is that a species can be doomed to die out long before the last survivor has disappeared. This happens because species need a minimum population size in order to remain reproductively viable. Many animals on today's endangered list are down to such low numbers that they would be certain to die out if they did not receive human help.

REJECT AND REPLACE

* *On at least five occasions in the earth's history, global cataclysms have wiped out huge numbers of species in a short space of time.* But when life is proceeding 'normally' – between such across-the-board disasters – extinction is a rare event. Perhaps half a dozen species die out each year, most of them small and highly localized animals such as land snails. For mammals and birds, the background extinction rate may be as low as half a dozen species every century. This low rate of extinction means there is plenty of time for new species to evolve, making up for the ones that lose out.

diplodocus

great auk

OBLIVION'S LIST

✱ In the last four centuries, however, the annual extinction rate has taken off. Over 200 species of birds and mammals are known to have died out in this period, including the flightless great auk, at least ten marsupials, an African antelope called the bluebuck, and Steller's sea cow. This giant relative of today's manatees weighed up to ten tonnes, making it the biggest casualty in recent history. *The list also includes at least 400 species of plants, 20 reptiles and two dozen species of fish*.

✱ These figures include only those extinctions that have been recorded. They are fairly reliable in the case of vertebrates, because these animals are generally conspicuous enough to be missed. They are less reliable for plants, and very unreliable for invertebrates. This is because the majority of invertebrates are too small to attract attention, and often live in inaccessible places. Many ecologists believe that if these were included the current extinction rate could <u>BE A DOZEN OR MORE SPECIES EACH DAY</u>.

✱ *This plunge in diversity cannot be put down to 'natural' causes. It has been triggered by an unprecedented biological phenomenon: the explosive rise of a single dominant species – the human race.*

Back from the dead?

According to science fiction films like *Jurassic Park*, scientists may one day be able to bring extinct species back to life. The likelihood of this actually happening is extremely slim, and the likelihood of the species becoming successfully re-established even slimmer. Without their original habitats, 'resurrected' species would stand little chance of survival.

when did I last make anything extinct?

human beings are the major cause of present-day extinctions

KEY WORDS

EXTINCTION: the disappearance of a species or group of species. Extinction usually occurs because species fail to adapt to changes in their environment.

CHAPTER 3

A SPECIES APART

* Palaeoecology - the ecological study of Earth's history - shows that our most distant ancestors had a negligible effect on their environment. They left few traces of themselves, and almost none of their impact on other species. The transformation from this low-impact lifestyle to the one we lead today came about through three crucial innovations: toolmaking, farming and industrialization.

archaeological rema are an important source of ecologic information

ancient tools

MAKING TOOLS

The age of wood

Many palaeontologists think that wooden tools, such as digging sticks and clubs, would have played a more important part in early Stone Age life than stone itself. Because wood slowly breaks down – like all organic matter – few of these 'Wood Age' tools survive.

ancient wooden objects have not survived

* Toolmaking is not unique to the human family. Chimps can make a variety of implements, from probes for extracting termites to sponges for collecting water. Even birds – despite being the proverbial dim-wits of the animal world – occasionally make simple tools to get at food. But, in the line leading to our species, toolmaking seems to have snowballed through a form of evolutionary feedback, with each advance opening the way for the next.

* At first, this feedback worked slowly, and innovations were few and far between. Our immediate ancestors – who belonged to a species called *Homo erectus*

– were proficient toolmakers, but they were not great inventors. We don't know what they managed to make out of wood, leather or bone, or what they might have done with the finished products. *However, progress in stone toolmaking was – by any standards – agonizingly slow. In one area of East Africa, only four new designs appeared in the space of a million years.*

TECHNOLOGY ON TRIAL

caveman

✱ More than two million years separated the beginning of the toolmaking era – mankind's original technological revolution – from the beginning of agriculture. Only 10,000 years separated the start of agriculture from the early days of industrialization, while just three centuries stand between the start of industrialization and today.

✱ *From an ecological perspective, these rapidly shrinking dates have important implications. They mean that farming still rates as a relatively recent experiment, even though it goes back to prehistoric times. Industrial living, with its much briefer track record, has had even less time to prove itself. Both have served the interests of the human species, but their long-term effects have not yet been fully felt.*

HUMANS AND HOMINIDS

Humans and our direct ancestors are collectively known as <u>HOMINIDS</u>. The earliest known hominids were the <u>AUSTRALOPITHECINES</u> (literally, 'southern apes'), which lived in Africa from about four million years ago. It is not known if australopithecines made stone tools. If they did, their tools were probably so simple that they would now be very difficult to distinguish from naturally chipped and broken stones. The oldest known toolmakers belonged to a species called *Homo habilis* ('handy man'), which superseded the australopithecines over 2.5 million years ago.

chimpanzees sometimes use tools

MOVING ON

* Even with rudimentary tools, our immediate ancestors had a much bigger impact on other animals than they would have had with muscle power alone. When our own species - *Homo*

prehistoric humans were excellent hunters

sapiens - appeared, tools and increased intelligence made humans formidable predators, able to tackle animals many times their own size. The remains of thousands of horses, found at Solutre in France, show that the slaughter could be immense.

LIGHTING UP

There is no clear evidence about exactly when our ancestors started to use fire. Among the earliest signs are layers of ash found at Zhoukoudian Cave in China. These date back about half a million years, to a time when the cave was inhabited by *Homo erectus*, the species that preceded humans. Making fire – as opposed to starting it from a natural blaze – is a much more recent skill. It probably started less than 25,000 years ago.

the Chinese were the first to make fire

TRAVELLING LIGHT

* The Solutré horses met their end about 17,000 years ago, when northern Europe was still in the grip of the last Ice Age. *By this fairly late stage in human prehistory, people were starting to have a major impact on the animals they hunted, driving some of them towards extinction.* Many palaeontologists suspect that HUMANS WERE INVOLVED IN A WAVE OF EXTINCTIONS that took place in North America about 11,000 years ago. This killed off three-quarters of the continent's large mammals, including the mammoth and woolly rhinoceros, and almost certainly had knock-on effects on the continent's plant life.

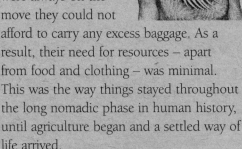

hunter-gatherer

* However, in one respect at least, the human impact was limited. Because people were always on the move they could not afford to carry any excess baggage. As a result, their need for resources – apart from food and clothing – was minimal. This was the way things stayed throughout the long nomadic phase in human history, until agriculture began and a settled way of life arrived.

THE LAST HUNTER-GATHERERS

* Fifty years ago, anthropologists could study people who still followed a lifestyle based on hunting and gathering wild food, much like that of our distant forebears. These people included – among others – the Australian Aborigines, the Chukchis of north-eastern Siberia, and the !Kung San or 'Bushmen' of the Kalahari Desert (the ! is a sharp clicking sound made with the back of the tongue). Today, very few true hunter-gatherers are left. Many !Kung San, for example, work as farm-hands in Botswana's cattle ranches – work that Australia's Aborigines have also taken up. *This ancient lifestyle looks almost certain to disappear in the 21st century.*

Sudden death

Opinions differ as to exactly why so many species of large North American mammals disappeared about 11,000 years ago. Some experts put it down to a sudden change in climate as the last Ice Age came to an end, while others think that it was entirely due to humans, coinciding with their arrival overland from Siberia. The jury is still out – not least because new archaeological clues hint that humans might have arrived in North America over 25,000 years ago – much earlier than previously thought.

up until 50 years ago there were still hunter-gatherers

straw

CULTURE CLUB

* The start of farming, about 10,000 years ago, triggered a social revolution for the human species, and an environmental revolution for the world as a whole. By planting and harvesting crops, people could store surplus food, allowing them to give up their wandering way of life. With this settled existence came new needs - ones that could have a major impact on their surroundings.

the Natufians of the Middle East were the earliest farmers

Need and greed

Farming has often been blamed for the materialism in human society because it gave people something worth hoarding and squabbling about – stored food. It also allowed the start of commerce, with some people living by providing goods and services, and others by growing food.

HARVEST TIME

* Farming began in an area of the Middle East known as the Fertile Crescent, although it later started independently in other parts of the world as well. *Among the pioneers of agriculture were the Natufians, a people who lived in the area covering present-day Israel and Lebanon.* Initially, the Natufians were semi-nomadic hunter-gatherers, harvesting wild grain using sickles made of sharpened stone, but about 11,000 years ago they began to sow wild grain as well.

Why they and other hunter-gatherers went to this trouble isn't known, because compared with a foraging lifestyle, producing food yourself is much harder work. Increasing population, together with changes in climate, have both been suggested as the cause.

SALT OF THE EARTH

✱ Natufian agriculture depended on rain, which limited how much food could be grown. But, by about 5,000 years ago, a much more sophisticated form of farming was developed by the Sumerians, who lived in Mesopotamia – an area that now forms part of Iraq. They irrigated their farmland, using water drawn from the Tigris and Euphrates rivers.

✱ *Sumerian temple records – which remarkably still survive – show that their harvests were initially far better than anything the Natufians could have achieved*. But as the centuries passed, the yields began to drop. By 1700 BC they were so poor that much of the land was abandoned, and the Sumerian civilization collapsed. Although they didn't know it, the Sumerian farmers had triggered ONE OF THE EARLIEST ENVIRONMENTAL CRISES IN HISTORY. By irrigating the land, they inadvertently dissolved salt deep within the soil. When the irrigation water evaporated in the hot summer sunshine, it left the salt behind as a hard crust. This problem – called salinization – still affects farming today.

Riches in rubbish

According to the 'dump heap theory', the first plants to be grown as crops came from campsite rubbish dumps containing rotting food and animal remains. These fertile seed-beds would have been ideal for wild grasses, so starting the cycle of collection and selection that has produced the crops we know today.

COSYING UP

The area of land needed to support one person living by hunting and gathering varies from one part of the world to another. An average figure is about 26 square kilometres (ten square miles), but in arid regions like the interior of Australia it can be ten times that amount. Agriculture provides food in a much more efficient way, so many more people can live in the same area. In Mesopotamia, for example, the population reached about 11 people per square kilometre (28 per square mile) in 2000 BC.

CLEARING THE GROUND

✴ As the first farmers discovered, growing crops isn't just a matter of scattering seeds and then waiting for the harvest. Before you can begin, you need to clear a suitable patch of land. When farming spread to regions that were covered by forest, land clearance brought about major environmental changes - a process that continues today.

they'll grow soon

european bison

Poland's primeval forest

Bialowieza Forest, on the border of Poland and Belarus, is one of the few large areas of original forest left in Europe. Once reserved as a royal hunting ground, the forest is now a World Heritage Site which draws thousands of visitors every year. Top of the list of attractions is a herd of European bison – a slimmed-down equivalent of the American species – which once roamed throughout Europe's forests. Today there are only a few hundred of these animals left.

HATCHET JOB

✴ Even with the simple technology of 5,000 years ago, land clearance could be surprisingly rapid. Just how rapid was shown by some experiments carried out by Danish archaeologists in the 1960s. Three men set about clearing an area of birch wood, using their hands and genuine Stone Age axes. After just four hours, they managed to clear about 600 square metres (6,500 square feet), cutting down the trees and burning their trunks and branches.

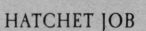

even with primitive tools, land clearance i a quick business

this pollen is from an oak tree

* When iron axe heads became available, from about 1000 BC in Europe, forest clearance became even faster. The wood that was felled was often turned into charcoal and used for smelting more iron, providing an extra incentive for cutting down yet more trees.

botanists can establish from which trees pollen comes

NORTH AND SOUTH

* *In North America, forest clearance began in the 1600s* – recently enough for it to form part of recorded history. Elsewhere in the northern hemisphere, it happened so long ago that it is hard to imagine how extensive the forest originally was. Taken as a whole, it shrank by about three-fifths, but in some areas – including the British Isles – it fell by up to 90%. With the forest went much of the wildlife, including deer, bears and wolves.

* *In the tropics, forest clearance has worked on a different time-scale. In Central America and New Guinea, archaeologists have found some evidence of clearance going back at least 7,000 years, but until 1900 equatorial rainforests remained largely intact. Since then, things have changed dramatically. About 40% of the rainforest cover has now gone, partly to clear land for farming, but also to produce timber. Under the onslaught of chain-saws and bulldozers rather than Stone Age axes, tropical rainforest is disappearing faster than any forest before it.*

POLLEN ANALYSIS

Even when forests are long gone, palynology – the science of pollen analysis – can show where they once were, and what trees they contained. Despite their tiny size, pollen grains are extremely durable, and can stay intact for thousands of years after being buried. The shape of pollen grains is as characteristic as a fingerprint, allowing botanists to establish which trees shed them, and often when they were released.

dust from the American prairies blew all the way to Washington

Blown away

'There was something fantastic about a dust cloud that covered 1.35 million square miles, stood three miles high and stretched from Canada to Texas, from Montana to Idaho... masses of dust began to billow into huge tumbling clouds, ebony black at the base and muddy tan at the top, some so saturated with dust particles that ducks and geese caught in flight suffocated; some turning the sky so black that chickens, thinking it was night, would roost.'

A CONTEMPORARY ACCOUNT OF THE GREAT DUST STORM THAT OCCURRED IN THE AMERICAN MIDWEST IN MAY 1934

MOTHER EARTH

mother

* The invention of the plough - yet another agricultural breakthrough to be credited to the Sumerians - dramatically increased the amount of land under cultivation because it allowed animal power to be put to work. It also did something else. By loosening the ground, early ploughs exposed the soil to erosion, a problem that farmland has suffered from ever since.

the Sumerians invented the plough

STRIPPING THE LAND

* Soil might look like a permanent feature in the landscape, but wind and rain erode it all the time. The rate of soil loss depends on the amount of plant cover there is, because PLANTS PROTECT SOIL by binding it together with their roots. In undisturbed forest – the best protected environment of all – an area the size of a football pitch can lose about 10kg (22lb) of soil a year, which works out at less than the thickness of a sheet of paper. This loss is balanced by new soil, created partly by the weathering of the bedrock below.

I've lost some soil have you seen it?

* When land is ploughed up, wind and rain can get at the soil, and erosion goes through the roof. In the United States and Europe, the amount of soil lost annually by an average piece of agricultural land – still the size of a football pitch – is nearly 14 tonnes. *In other parts of the world, particularly in places with dry climates, the figure can be as high as 50 tonnes.* At this rate, soil that took thousands of years to build up is rapidly stripped away.

DUST BOWL YEARS

* *Soil erosion has been described as one of the greatest but least noticed threats facing mankind.* While most people lose no sleep over it, there have been times when its harmful effects have been impossible to avoid. In recent history, the worst episode of erosion took place during the 1930s, when the ploughed-up prairies of the American Midwest dried up and blew away. According to reports from the time, one storm dropped dust onto ships in the Atlantic, and onto the President's desk in Washington, 2,400km (1,500 miles) away.

WALKING ON RUST

Erosion isn't the only man-made change that can have harmful effects on the ground. SALINIZATION (pages 86–7) makes land toxic to most plants, while LATERIZATION gives it a surface like concrete, so that very little can take root. Laterization happens only in the tropics, on red soils that are rich in iron. When these soils are exposed, the iron forms a rust-like crust on the surface.

soil erosion makes it impossible to grow anything

ANIMAL FARM

a-hunting we will go...

✱ Plants were not the only living things that hunter-gatherers eventually brought under their control. From about 12,000 years ago, dogs joined them in the hunt, driving animals towards places where they were easy to attack. Once hunters had learnt how to round up herds, managing the way they lived was just a short step away.

dogs were domesticated about 12,000 years ago

HERD MENTALITY

**✱ *The domestication of the dog, from its ancestor the grey wolf, probably happened somewhere in southern Asia.* A couple of thousand years later, people learnt how to control wild sheep – the first animals to be actively managed as a source of food. Sheep have two features that make them ideal candidates for domestication: they rarely turn nasty, and they hardly ever wander off on their own. At a time when predators were common and fences non-existent, the second was a major plus.

✱ In the Middle East, three other species became domesticated during the next**

Elephant power

Since agriculture first began, about 50 different animals have been domesticated. The most important are mammals and birds, but they also include fish and a handful of insects – notably the silkworm and honeybee. The largest domesticated animal by a long way is the elephant. Today, working elephants are found only in Asia, but in historical times, the larger African elephant was also used as a beast of burden. In his legendary assault on Rome, the Carthaginian general Hannibal is reputed to have crossed the Alps with a regiment of war elephants. How many of them made it back home is not known.

the African elephant

wild boar

three millennia: the wild goat, the wild boar, and the aurochs – the ancestor of today's cattle. Compared with sheep and goats, wild boar and aurochs could be aggressive and dangerous. *Part of the domestication process involved breeding from the tamest individuals, until most of this aggression was eventually weeded out.*

CAPTIVE COUSINS

✱ Farther north, in eastern Europe and Central Asia, **wild horses were also brought under human control.** Initially raised for food, they were soon being used for their muscle power as well. As domesticated horses spread, their wild counterparts became progressively more rare, until they almost completely died out.

✱ *A small number of wild horses did manage to survive, although they came perilously close to extinction.* Several other domesticated species, such as the chicken and turkey, became rare in the wild, while the numbers of their captive counterparts shot up. However, for the aurochs – ancestor of probably the most important domestic animal of all – domestication spelt the end of life in the wild. It created the ultimate competitor: an animal that ate the same food, often in the same habitat, but which had humans on its side.

PLANET CHICKEN

The most abundant domesticated animal is the chicken – a descendant of the jungle fowl of Southeast Asia. Chickens are thought to have been domesticated about 5,000 years ago, possibly in India. Today the world's chicken population is estimated to be nearly ten billion, turning out about 500 billion eggs a year.

there's more of us chickens than there are of you

chickens are the most numerous domesticated animal

cattle-ranching
had a far-reaching
environmental
impact

HOME ON THE RANGE

* In folklore, the shepherd tending his flock - or the cowboy on his horse - are celebrated as figures living in harmony with the land. But from an ecological point of view the real story is rather different. Since people first started raising animals, over 10,000 years ago, hungry herds have had some profound effects on the world's landscapes.

shepherd

94

INTO THE BREACH

* A striking example of their effects can be seen in the islands of the Aegean Sea. Here, not far from where goats and sheep were first domesticated, the original vegetation was a form of evergreen woodland adapted to the climate of wet winters and long, dry summers. Most of the trees were cut down for timber many centuries ago and, at the same time, goats were raised for food. *The goats nibbled away at young saplings, preventing the woodland from re-establishing itself, and without the trees the winter rain washed much of the soil away.*

* Goats are notoriously unfussy eaters, but there are some plants they will not touch. Among them are spurges — plants that have a poisonous fiery-tasting sap.

cooked chicken

The goats ate up the spurges' competitors, allowing them to spread. As a result, these inedible plants are much more common than they were before the goats arrived.

✱ Sheep and goats are not the only animals capable of producing this kind of environmental change. In the cattle-ranching country of the western USA, livestock numbers increased rapidly at the end of the 19th century. Their browsing encouraged the spread of burrow-weed, another poisonous plant, as well as inedible shrubs such as sagebrush and mesquite. The more cattle the land supports, the more common these plants become.

barbed wire divided up the West

NEW OPPORTUNITIES

✱ In ecological jargon, this phenomenon is known as <u>COMPETITIVE RELEASE</u>. It happens whenever a species is suddenly freed from one of the factors that normally keeps it under control. When crops are sprayed with pesticides it's not unusual for one pest to benefit from another's demise, triggering off a chain reaction that only further pesticides can halt.

Second-hand food

Compared with growing plants, raising animals is a very inefficient way of producing food. This is because it inserts an extra link in the food chain (pages 28–9), and that extra link means that a large amount of the original food energy is lost. Where animals are farmed intensively, it can take 15kg of feed to produce 1kg of beef, and 3kg of feed to produce 1kg of chicken or turkey.

THE GREAT DIVIDE

The invention of barbed wire, in 1873, was one of the most important developments in animal husbandry. It meant that open rangeland – like the American West and the Australian Outback – could be divided up into lots quickly and cheaply. It also meant that cattle could be concentrated in particular areas, increasing their impact on the vegetation.

ADDED EXTRAS

✱ Since agriculture began, soil erosion is estimated to have put a third of the world's cultivated ground out of action, including most of the land that the Sumerians originally tilled. But cultivation hasn't all been a one-way process. Over the centuries, farmers have added a wide range of substances to the ground - with both good and bad results.

soil improvement is an important business

SICK SOIL

Rock bottom

Unlike nitrogen, phosphate still has to be extracted from the ground. Today, most of it comes from the United States, Russia and North Africa, but until recently a significant amount came from the tiny Pacific island of Nauru, one of the world's smallest independent nations. Nauru is – or more accurately was – almost solid phosphate-bearing rock. Most of it has now been removed by mining, creating a completely uninhabitable lunar landscape on which nothing can grow.

DESIRABLE DROPPINGS

✱ These additives have included lime and marl (a form of lime-rich clay), shells, seaweed, ground-up bones, and manure of every conceivable kind. Bird-droppings were popular with the ancient Egyptians and Greeks, and the dried bird-droppings industry underwent a short but spectacular boom in the 19th century. *Horse manure was also big business, since there was an awful lot of it. In 19th-century Paris it was used to fertilize*

the more you put in, the more you get out

gardens around the city, where the warmth from decomposition helped to produce up to six crops of vegetables a year.

FIXED BY FRITZ

✱ Until the 20th century, fertilizers were all based on natural substances. Selected by trial and error, they contain high CONCENTRATIONS OF NITROGEN OR PHOSPHORUS – two elements that plants need for growth. *Natural fertilizers can be smelly and unmanageable*, but for most of agricultural history there was nothing else that farmers could use. That changed in 1913, when the chemist **Fritz Haber** discovered a way of artificially 'fixing' nitrogen from the air to make ammonia. His process was initially harnessed to make explosives but, after the Second World War, fertilizer production took off, rapidly increasing to over 100 million tonnes a year.

✱ *Artificial fertilizers – together with improved crops – have had a tremendous impact on world food production.* However, they do have some major drawbacks. One is that they are easily washed away by rain, contaminating rivers and drinking water. Another is that they don't contain any organic matter – material that can sustain the teeming life within the soil. Without this organic input, the soil's biological health slowly goes downhill.

ou se trouve la merde, il y a aussi l'argent...

THE GUANO TRADE

During the mid-19th century, a cluster of arid islands off the coast of Peru became the centre of one of the world's most unusual export businesses, based on seabird droppings. Over thousands of years, the droppings had built up to form guano, a natural fertilizer packed with nitrogen and phosphorus. In just 30 years, over ten million tons of guano were shipped to Europe and the USA. Eventually the resource was exhausted, and the trade collapsed.

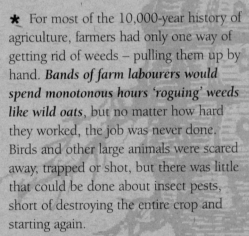

I'll be glad when chemical weedkillers are invented

CLEAN SWEEP

* In the 18th and 19th centuries, a series of innovations - from crop rotation to new machinery - brought about a steady intensification of agriculture, as farming became a more scientific business. Even so, farmland still teemed with wildlife, because pests and weeds were very difficult to eradicate. After the Second World War, this rapidly changed.

extremely deadly →

WHITE ARSENIC

ARSENIC AND OLD LACE

At the beginning of the 20th century, the chemicals used to clear farmland weeds were often highly toxic to both plant and animal life. They included white arsenic (arsenic trioxide), a substance that can be deadly if inhaled, and which is also carcinogenic. Because white arsenic is odourless and tasteless, it was once a favourite with would-be poisoners.

WAR ON WEEDS

* For most of the 10,000-year history of agriculture, farmers had only one way of getting rid of weeds – pulling them up by hand. *Bands of farm labourers would spend monotonous hours 'roguing' weeds like wild oats*, but no matter how hard they worked, the job was never done. Birds and other large animals were scared away, trapped or shot, but there was little that could be done about insect pests, short of destroying the entire crop and starting again.

* In the late 1800s, chemists discovered a number of substances that would kill plants, so that ground could be completely cleared. They also discovered the first SELECTIVE HERBICIDES – substances that kill particular plants while leaving others more or less unharmed. Most of these were based on inorganic substances such as sulphur, copper and iron, and had to be used in large quantities to have any effect. But during the late 1940s a completely new group of herbicides became available. Made from organic substances, they were lethal to weeds in tiny amounts. Flower-filled fields and weed-choked pastures soon became a thing of the past.

> ## KEY WORDS
>
> **MONOCULTURE:** a form of agriculture in which a single species is grown in an area to the exclusion of everything else

modern weedkillers meant the end of poppy fields

TOTAL EXCLUSION ZONES

★ This breakthrough in weed control coincided with the development of new ORGANIC PESTICIDES, such as chlordane, dieldrin and DDT. *Together, herbicides and pesticides helped to bring about what earlier farmers could only have dreamed about*: true monocultures, or fields that contain crop plants and nothing else.

★ Unfortunately, as the following years have shown, there is an ecological price to be paid for such effective forms of weed and pest control. Many of the plants and animals that were formerly common in farmland have become rare, and some have been pushed to the edge of extinction.

Silent Spring revisited

Rachel Carson's warnings about pesticide use (pages 10–11) have been borne out by a steep drop in the numbers of songbirds in many parts of the world. Some of this is due to habitat loss but, for many species, modern farming practices are equally to blame. Today's herbicides and pesticides rarely harm birds directly – unlike the first-generation products of the 40s and 50s – but they do kill the plants and animals that small songbirds need as food. Without this food, fewer of the birds can survive.

I'm off

THE GREEN REVOLUTION

* In the late 1950s, high-intensity agriculture began to spread to the countries of the developing world. This marked the start of the Green Revolution - a 30-year period of soaring harvests that saw many poor countries becoming self-sufficient in food. With this steep rise in production came an increasing dependence on agricultural chemicals - and ecological problems on a global scale.

it's a *miracle*

miracle rice
the Philippin

Joining the resistance

One shortcoming of pesticides is that they have a scatter-gun effect. In the ensuing shoot-out, the good guys – natural predators of pests – get killed along with the bad guys. Another problem is that the chemicals actively encourage resistance to their effects. This happens because, in any species, individuals have variations in their genes. In any population of pests, a few are likely to have genes that give them natural resistance to a particular pesticide – and, if that pesticide is used repeatedly, the non-resistant individuals die out while the resistant ones rapidly multiply.

THE GREAT LEAP FORWARD

* *The Green Revolution started in Mexico*, shortly after the end of the Second World War. Plant breeders funded by the Rockefeller Foundation created new strains of wheat which gave spectacularly high yields – as long as they were grown in the right conditions. In the 1960s, the same thing happened with rice. 'Miracle rice' produced double or even triple the yields that farmers would normally expect.

can't get rid of me that easy

100

The effect on food production was phenomenal, particularly in the developing world. India was able to build up its own food reserves instead of relying on grain from abroad, and **Mexico's grain output increased eight-fold in 20 years.**

Mexicans had never had it so good

FINGERS CROSSED

✱ In human terms, the Green Revolution ranks as one of the 20th century's greatest achievements, providing extra food at a time of urgent need. From an ecological standpoint, its record is not so good. The new miracle crops came as part of a package which needed fertilizers and pesticides in order to work. As a result, global use of agricultural CHEMICALS ROSE EVEN FASTER THAN HARVESTS. By the late 1960s, nearly half a million tonnes of DDT had built up in the environment, much of it scattered onto high-yield crops.

✱ Although today's pesticides are less dangerous than DDT, another major ecological problem remains. High-intensity farming has increased our RELIANCE ON A HANDFUL OF CROP VARIETIES, instead of the many thousands that farmers once raised. In the long run this collapse in biodiversity is bad news, because it means that many old varieties – with useful features like disease resistance – may disappear. And, once they have gone, their genetic potential is lost forever.

GREEN GIANTS

In the 19th century, wheat plants often grew chest-high – tall enough to provide long stalks that could be used for thatching roofs. But with cereals like wheat, bigger isn't necessarily better: 19th-century wheat wasted a lot of energy in growing stalks rather than grain, and it was easily flattened by storms. One of the breakthroughs of the Green Revolution was to create semi-dwarf varieties of wheat and rice. Although shorter, these plants produce more food.

roof thatcher

101

this tomato could grow in the Arctic

genetic engineer

JUMPING GENES

✱ During the Green Revolution, new crop strains were created by reshuffling the genes already present in rice or wheat - a 20th-century version of techniques thousands of years old. But, in the 1980s, a new and much more precise way of modifying plants became available. Unlike traditional breeding techniques, genetic engineering can move genes between species, providing unprecedented power to change living things.

'Sadly, much of the discussion about biotechnology has been dominated by scaremongering and wildly inaccurate but highly emotional language...
Claims that animal and fish genes have been put into plants have been used to convince consumers that their food is unsafe and unnatural.'

ANN FOSTER, SPOKESPERSON FOR MONSANTO, A LEADING BIOTECHNOLOGY COMPANY

MIX 'N' MATCH

✱ The techniques involved in genetic engineering are complex, but the possibilities they open up are extraordinary. Within certain limits, genetic engineering allows almost any gene to be copied from one species and inserted into another. Because genes operate through a universal chemical code shared by all living things, each one will function wherever it ends up – in a bacterium, a plant, or a human being.

✱ For plant breeders, the benefits of genetic engineering are immense. It's fast, it's dazzlingly precise, and it allows plants to be given CHARACTERISTICS THAT THEY HAVE NEVER HAD BEFORE. Any useful feature coded by a single gene – such

genetic engineering is
the best thing to
happen to us

as disease resistance,
tolerance to cold, or
toxicity to pests –
can be picked out and transferred, creating
new 'transgenic' crops.

BRAVE NEW WORLD

✱ Advocates of genetic engineering
argue that it is the best thing that has
happened to agriculture since the
Green Revolution got under way.
Some believe that it is even
more important than this –
making it perhaps the
most significant
development since farming
began. However, many
environmentalists do not
share these upbeat views. They see genetic
engineering as an economic threat to
farmers, and a source of ecological danger.
✱ The economic threat comes from the
power that major agrochemical companies
will have as they patent new varieties of
the world's staple crops. The ecological
danger is that transgenic plants might
behave in unpredictable ways, particularly
if they escape into the wild. If their new
genes are passed on to wild plants, this
could create sudden instability in natural
ecosystems, with hybrid plants running
riot. It's a fear that genetic engineers
dismiss, but with biotechnology still in its
infancy, no one yet knows if their
confidence is well placed.

KEY WORDS

TRANSGENIC:
a word used to describe
any organism whose
genetic make-up has
been artificially altered
to include genes from
other species

will genetic
engineering
put small
farmers out of
business?

'The five major
agrochemical
companies envisage
a future where
only a handful of
varieties of...
crops are grown
commercially. They
are working flat
out now to ensure
that within a
decade most of
the world's staple
crops will be from
genetically
modified seeds
which they have
engineered.'

PATRICK HOLDEN,
UK SOIL ASSOCIATION

CHAPTER 4

THE PEOPLE PLANET

* For most of human history, the world's population has crept upwards at an almost imperceptible rate. During the 1300s it even went into reverse, as millions of people died during the Black Death, a global outbreak of bubonic plague. But with the start of the Industrial Age, about 250 years ago, the brakes were released. Human numbers went into an exponential climb - which is only now starting to slacken.

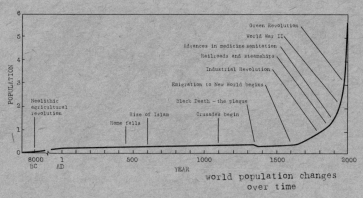

world population changes over time

Changing gear

The current fall in the world's population growth rate is largely the result of a change from high birth rates and high death rates to lower rates for both. This process is known as a <u>DEMOGRAPHIC TRANSITION</u>. During a demographic transition, the fall in the birth rate comes about several generations after the fall in the death rate, creating a period of very rapid growth.

GOING UP

* Even for the most ardent fans of the human species, the figures make uncomfortable reading. At the beginning of the 20th century there were about 1.6 billion people on Earth. By the end of it, the numbers have risen to 6 billion – over a million times as many as when agriculture first began. The effects of natural disasters, two world wars, and an endless catalogue of other conflicts, have been shrugged off in a seemingly unstoppable upward surge.

* The causes of this steep growth are more complex than they first seem. The POPULATION EXPLOSION is often put down to modern medicine, but it actually began before the era of modern drugs or mass immunization. Overall, a more important factor was an improving food supply, together with better hygiene and sanitation. Once these were in place, 20th-century developments – including the discovery of antibiotics and the Green Revolution – fuelled an increase that was already under way.

THE S-CURVE

* Charts of human population growth look very much like the ones produced during ecological experiments, when animals reproduce without any of the checks that normally hold them back. *Just like a flour beetle colony, the human population has taken time to get into its exponential phase, and that part of the growth cycle can only last a certain time.* In the 1950s and 1960s the curve was still getting steeper, but in recent years there have been signs that it is beginning to fall back.

* According to recent estimates, that fall suggests that the population will stabilize at around 12 billion about 100 years from now. *The crucial question is whether that figure will exceed the Earth's carrying capacity for the human species.*

KEY WORDS

DEMOGRAPHIC TRANSITION:
a reduction in population growth rate, generally attributed to increasing economic development

Stuck in the middle

In most developed countries the demographic transition is now complete, but in many developing countries it is still under way. In Africa, in particular, death rates have fallen, but birth rates are still high. As a result, many of these countries have growth rates of over 3%.

birth rates in Africa
are still high

105

Paul Ehrlich

IT'S OFFICIAL

In 1972, Paul Ehrlich's warnings on the effects of population growth were echoed in *The Limits to Growth*, a report commissioned by a group of business leaders called the Club of Rome. The report spelled out the dangers of unlimited population increase, and recommended immediate action to combat pollution and rein in industrial growth. In 1981, similar action was recommended by the *Global 2000 Report to the President*, an official report commissioned by the US Government.

the boomsters group

DOOM OR BOOM?

* In 1968, when human numbers were growing faster than ever before, the American biologist Paul Ehrlich published a book called *The Population Bomb*. Ehrlich warned that humanity was about to 'breed itself into oblivion'. His dire warnings triggered an often acrimonious debate between ecological 'doomsters', like Ehrlich himself, and the 'boomsters' - a group of economists with much more upbeat views.

MAN WITH A MISSION

* *The Population Bomb* made grim reading. In it, Ehrlich argued that the Earth already held far more people than it could support, and that, within decades, starvation would set population growth into reverse. By the end of the century, the high standard of living enjoyed by people in the developed world would be a distant memory. Despite its doom-laden message – or perhaps because of it – Ehrlich's book became a best-seller.

we are breedir into oblivior

✱ In the years immediately after the book was published, events seemed to bear out Ehrlich's views. **The population boom continued, and the Arab–Israeli War of 1973 resulted in an Arab oil embargo against the West.** Fuel was rationed and unemployment rose, creating widespread anxiety about the future.

DOOMSDAY POSTPONED

✱ But things didn't work out quite as Ehrlich had predicted. The world's population continued to grow without triggering any of the cataclysmic events that he insisted would follow. Instead, quite the reverse happened: during the 1980s the world economy boomed.

✱ Where had Ehrlich gone wrong? For economists like **Julian Simon**, author of a book called *Population Matters*, the answer was clear: people are a resource – one that Ehrlich had ignored. According to this 'cornucopian' argument, more people means a higher level of economic growth, which in turn produces an improved quality of life.

✱ Simon's arguments have attracted support, particularly after some highly successful predictions of his own (see pages 110–11). For their part, many environmentalists concede that Ehrlich may have been unduly alarmist, but they remain convinced that the burden of his argument – that we are <u>MULTIPLYING TOO FAST FOR OUR OWN GOOD</u> – still holds true.

opinions differ as to whether we are reproducing too quickly

'The battle to feed humanity is over. In the 1970s...hundreds of millions of people are going to starve to death...nothing can prevent a substantial increase in the world death rate...America's vast agricultural surpluses are gone.'

PAUL EHRLICH, IN *THE POPULATION BOMB*

107

INDUSTRIAL EARTH

✴ On its own, the size of the human population doesn't determine our collective impact on the environment. An equally important factor is the way people live. No matter how 'green' you are, if you live in an industrialized nation, using resources and creating pollution are inescapable facts of life.

recycling helps, but industrialized societies always have a high environmental impact

MAKING A MARK

what am I going to do with all this lot?!

Norwegians are the world's biggest consumers because of their huge fishing industry

✴ Since the Industrial Age began, human lifestyles have begun to diverge, so that some people now have a far greater environmental impact than others. Ecologists sum this up in the 'impact equation', which is written as $I = P \times T$. The two factors on the right-hand side of the equation are population and technology. Multiply them together and you get the one on the left – a figure for total human environmental impact.

✴ When the figures are filled in, each country produces different results. In global terms, the population figures for most industrialized countries come some way down the list, but in all of them the

I can't believe the
Norwegians beat us!

technology factor looms large. As a result, the total environmental impact of their citizens is very high. In developing countries the technology factor is lower, but the population is often higher. When the maths is done, their total human impact is high as well.

HOW DO YOU RATE?

* A problem with the impact equation is that, in practice, it is not that easy to put into numerical form. Population figures are simple to get hold of, but technology is a much vaguer measurement, open to differences in interpretation. One way around this is to work it out from things that go hand in hand with technology such as consumption of raw materials.

* This approach was adopted by the World Wide Fund for Nature when it surveyed all the world's countries for its *Living Planet Report*, published in 1998. The report showed that if the world average consumer had an impact of 1, the average North American came in at 2.7, and the average Western European at 1.72. At the other end of the scale, the average African had a figure of just 0.55.

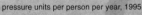

pressure units per person per year, 1995

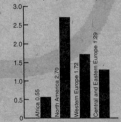

consumption pressure by region

WHO IS NUMBER 1?

In the WWF's *Living Planet report*, US citizens came sixth in the list of nations with top-scoring 'consumption pressures'. Beating them into the top five were – in ascending order – Danes, Singaporeans, Chileans, Taiwanese and Norwegians. These surprising results were produced by calculating the national consumption of five raw materials – grain, fish, wood, fresh water and cement – and the levels of one form of waste: carbon dioxide, produced by burning fuel. Norway captured the Number 1 slot thanks to its massive fish catch – equivalent to quarter of a tonne per Norwegian per year – and its high levels of carbon dioxide emissions.

THE TEN-YEAR TUSSLE

* According to 'cornucopian' economics, natural resources don't have any real limits, because human ingenuity will always come up with more effective ways of using them, or of finding replacements. Most ecologists believe that in the long term the opposite is true, which is one of the reasons we need to safeguard the resources that we have. In October 1980, a celebrated wager put these two viewpoints to the test.

Dash for cash

Can the human population be stabilized by world-wide development? Some of today's leading 'doomsters' think that the answer is no. They argue that many of today's densely populated developed countries function only because they can import resources from developing countries, which have little or no industry of their own. If these countries become industrialized, the supply of resources will dry up. 'Cornucopian' economists reject this idea, maintaining that free markets will provide all the resources we need.

we can always find new uses for natural resources

PUT UP OR SHUT UP

* The challenge was issued by **Julian Simon**, the prominent cornucopian economist. *He argued that if resources really are becoming scarcer – as ecologists assume they should be – market forces will mean that their cost will go up.* On the other hand, if the cornucopian view is right, the cost of resources should go down. Simon believed in the downward path, and he challenged anyone to prove him wrong.

stockmarket

* The biologist **Paul Ehrlich** agreed to take him on, and a public bet was arranged. It covered the prices of five industrial metals over ten years. The initial stock of metals was worth $1,000. If their price went up, Simon would pay Ehrlich the increase, but if it went down, Ehrlich would be out of pocket. In October 1990, the price of the five metals had fallen by almost half – even further if inflation was taken into account. Ehrlich duly paid up.

TRUST THE MARKET

* Since 1990, many economists – particularly in the USA – have used Simon's win to dismiss the idea that dwindling resources need ever be a problem for mankind, as long as market forces are allowed to have their way. They point out that compared with average wages, the cost of most natural resources is about half the level in 1950, and in the case of fossil fuels, new stocks are being discovered all the time. *According to this view, population growth creates wealth, and this wealth finances solutions to the problems that growth sometimes creates.*

* Comforting though it is, THIS SCENARIO HAS NOT MADE MANY CONVERTS AMONG ECOLOGISTS. Many agree that in the short term, resources may be plentiful enough. *But as we consume more and more we are creating major changes in the biosphere – changes that no amount of extra wealth will be able to correct.*

Hurry, while stocks last

Whales are a 'commodity' that highlights both sides of the argument about resources. From the mid-1700s, sperm whales were hunted for their oil – a clean-burning fuel that was used in candles and lamps. Up to 5,000 sperm whales were killed each year, but the species was reprieved when whale oil was replaced by kerosene – a classic example of resource substitution. However, with the larger baleen whales, which are hunted for their meat, there has been no substitution. Without international protection, market forces would almost certainly drive them to extinction.

sperm whale

UNFRIENDLY FIRE

✱ Of all the resources needed to keep modern lifestyles going, energy comes top of the list. Since the discovery of fossil fuels - which goes back well before industrial times - obtaining energy, and using it, have had a major impact on the world's ecosystems.

Hubbert's bubble

In 1956, the American geologist **M. King Hubbert** showed that production from any oilfield follows a bell-shaped curve. *The curve reaches its highest point when about half the oil is gone, creating a production peak called 'Hubbert's bubble'.* Many oil analysts today think that world oil production will peak around the year 2010 before beginning a steep descent.

humans use up more energy than other animals, mostly through burning fossil fuels

BEYOND THE BODY

✱ On average, an adult human body needs about 2,000 kilocalories of energy a day – about enough to bring three bucketfuls of water to the boil. If we were like other forms of life, that would be our total energy requirement, because living things can only use energy at a certain rate. But this 'SOMATIC' OR BODILY ENERGY is not the only kind that we use. Since the discovery of fire, it has been gradually eclipsed by extra-somatic energy – the kind we release in other ways. *For the mythical average person, this supplementary energy*

oil rig

coal miner

adds up to about 300,000
kilocalories per day, or 150 times the
amount our bodies actually need. Most of
it comes from fossil fuels – coal, oil and
natural gas.

PULLING THE PLUG

✱ At present rates of use, fossil fuels are
in no immediate danger of running out.
However, opinions differ sharply on how
long they can last. The Earth's coal
reserves are vast – enough to last at least
another two centuries – but proven
reserves of oil and gas are nothing like so
large. There is probably enough of both to
last 50 years at current rates, and further
reserves are certain to be found. Offsetting
this is the fact that consumption rates are
not steady. Instead, they are going up by
several per cent a year.

✱ But, before we actually run out of any
of these fuels, their harmful side-effects will
FORCE US TO LIMIT THEIR USE. All of them –
particularly coal – contain substances
that create poisonous gases when
they burn, but, even if these are
completely removed, fossil fuels
cause problems in another
way. They are prime culprits
in boosting the GREENHOUSE
EFFECT (see pages 146–47),
a phenomenon set to
become one of the 21st
century's greatest ,
environmental problems.

CREATIVE ACCOUNTING

Figures for the amount
of oil left to be
extracted are notoriously
unreliable and are prone
to political 'fixing'. In
the mid-1980s, for
example, many OPEC
countries – including
Saudi Arabia, Kuwait
and Venezuela –
announced that their
reserves had suddenly
increased by between
40% and 200%, even
though no major new
discoveries had been
made. This sudden
jump allowed them to
increase their export
quotas at a time when
they were theoretically
meant to be reining
back.

stopping the Earth from
overheating is one of
ecology's biggest challenges

113

Fission and fusion

Today's nuclear reactors work by **nuclear fission**. This releases heat and also gamma rays – a form of radiation so intense that it can only be blocked by several feet of concrete. An alternative way of releasing energy from atoms, called **nuclear fusion**, does not produce gamma rays or radioactive waste. However, fusion takes place only at temperatures of about 15,000,000°C. So far, physicists have been unable to make it work on a commercial scale.

FILL HER UP

One kilogram (2.2lb) of uranium fuel can release about the same amount of energy as two million litres (440,000 gallons) of petrol.

radioactive materials escaped from the reactor at Chernobyl

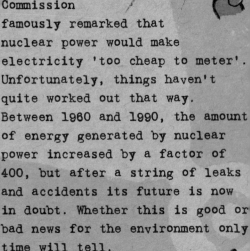

NUCLEAR POWER

✷ In 1954 the chairman of the US Atomic Energy Commission famously remarked that nuclear power would make electricity 'too cheap to meter'. Unfortunately, things haven't quite worked out that way. Between 1960 and 1990, the amount of energy generated by nuclear power increased by a factor of 400, but after a string of leaks and accidents its future is now in doubt. Whether this is good or bad news for the environment only time will tell.

PLUS AND MINUS

✷ Compared with conventional ways of generating energy, nuclear power has some big advantages. It runs on very small amounts of fuel and, because the fuel isn't burned, it doesn't release waste gases into the atmosphere. *It can be used by countries that have no fossil fuel resources, reducing the need for coal, oil or gas* to be moved from place to place.

✷ The downside of nuclear power is that it involves POTENTIALLY LETHAL

MATERIALS. Nuclear fuels are intensely radioactive, and the waste produced by nuclear fission is radioactive as well. If any of these materials escape from a reactor – as they did at Chernobyl in 1986 – they can create illness and environmental damage on a massive scale.

PULLING THE PLUG

✱ The Chernobyl disaster was the largest reactor accident in the history of nuclear power, and may have claimed over 5,000 lives. *In 1979, a potentially greater disaster, at Three Mile Island in Pennsylvania,* was averted only because nuclear fuel failed to melt through a reactor's steel and concrete walls. These two accidents, and a number of others, have given nuclear power its present dangerous reputation. Apart from France, few Western countries are commissioning new nuclear power plants, and some are giving up nuclear power altogether.

✱ However, if the entire world abandoned this source of energy, some other way would have to be found of generating 300 BILLION WATTS OF POWER – the amount that nuclear energy currently supplies. *Advocates of nuclear energy argue that this cannot be done without inflicting increased damage on the environment. For the anti-nuclear lobby, the risks are too great to make nuclear power worthwhile.*

KEY WORDS

NUCLEAR FISSION: the splitting of heavy atoms to produce lighter ones. During the process, the atoms lose a small amount of mass which becomes converted into energy.

NUCLEAR FUSION: the combining of light atoms to produce heavier ones. This process produces the energy released by the sun.

some scientists say that the risks from nuclear power are less than the dangers of drinking two cups of coffee per day

hydroelectric dam

ENERGY ON THE MOVE

* No smoke, no polluting gases, and best of all no hazardous waste - it sounds like the perfect way of solving the perennial energy problem. However, as many countries have found, big dams may produce lots of electricity, but they often bring environmental problems in their wake.

ELEMENTARY BLUNDERS

World-wide, there are now nearly 40,000 dams over 15m (50 feet) high, and hundreds of thousands of smaller ones. One of the shortest-lived was the San Men Xia Dam on China's Yellow River. The reservoir behind it filled with sediment just four years after the dam was built. Lake Nasser – the reservoir behind the Aswan High Dam – is expected to be half-filled with sediment by 2025.

MINE'S BIGGER THAN YOURS

* Dams have been used for generating power for over 2,000 years, although using them to drive generator turbines rather than waterwheels is a much more recent innovation. The first hydroelectric dam was built in 1889, and today about 15% of the world's running surface water runs up against a dam at some point on its journey back to the sea. *During the 20th century, giant dams became national status symbols. The Hoover Dam, built on the Colorado River, USA, between 1930 and 1936, created one of the world's biggest man-made lakes at over 180km (110 miles) long.* But, in 1970, Russian engineers working in Egypt went one better: when the

salmon

Aswan High Dam was completed, it impounded a lake over 350km (217 miles) long, containing about 170 cubic kilometres (40 cubic miles) of water.

WINNERS AND LOSERS

✱ The dam at Aswan has turned into a textbook example of how big dams can have UNWELCOME ECOLOGICAL RESULTS. Because the dam was built without large sluices, it holds back all the nutrient-rich silt that previously fertilized Egypt's farmland during the Nile's annual flood. Egyptian farmers now have to use artificial fertilizer instead. The dam also created a giant arena for ecological succession (see pages 44–5). Among the early winners in the ensuing scramble were freshwater snails – ones that transmit bilharzia, a parasitic disease that can infect humans. In other parts of the world, new reservoirs have become clogged by floating water-plants. These can sometimes build up to such numbers that they bring turbines to a halt.

✱ *Dams are bad news for land animals – particularly when forests are flooded – but they can also affect fish. Migrating salmon can pass dams by jumping up specially-built 'fish ladders', but not all fish are this athletic. Once a dam has been built, sluggish swimmers are cut off from their spawning grounds, and soon disappear.*

The 'New Dambusters'

In 1996, the Newport Number 11 dam on the Clyde River in Vermont became the first dam on record to be blown up for environmental reasons. The 5m (16-foot) dam had stood in the way of migrating salmon for four decades, but, within weeks of being destroyed, the salmon had recolonized the area upstream.

this is too energetic for me, I'm not going to bother this year

dams can prevent salmon from reaching their spawning grounds

SPLASHING OUT

* In the last 40 years, the Aral Sea in Central Asia - a giant lake once plied by fleets of fishing boats - has shrunk like a puddle drying out in the sun. Hit by an agricultural experiment which went badly wrong, it shows what can happen when humans treat water as a limitless resource.

THAT SINKING FEELING

When water is pumped out of underground aquifers, the water table slowly sinks, which means that wells have to be dug ever deeper to reach the water level. In some parts of Texas, the water table of the Ogallala Aquifer has sunk by 50m (165 feet) in the last half-century. In parts of the Australian outback, where agriculture depends on groundwater, it has fallen by 100m (330ft).

where has all the sea gone?

when rivers were diverted, the Aral Sea dried up

DRY TIMES

* The Aral Sea's problems began in the early 1960s, when Soviet planners decided that the land around it should be irrigated to grow cotton and other crops. So much water was diverted from the region's two main rivers that in summer only a trickle made it to its former destination. *Starved of its normal water supply, the Aral Sea began to disappear.* As the coast receded, former fishing ports were stranded many miles inland, and, to make matters worse, fertilizer-laden dust was blown off the dry lake bed, making living near the lake a major health hazard.

my hook's got stuck in the mud

sea snail

* The 'Aral experience' has been blamed on bureaucratic incompetence and a failure to understand the basic facts of the WATER CYCLE. But Soviet planners have not been alone in making basic ecological mistakes where water is concerned. In the USA, the Colorado River is almost empty by the time it reaches the sea, and the Ogallala Aquifer – a vast reservoir of groundwater beneath the High Plains states – may be pumped dry within the next 40 years.

EVAPORATING ASSETS

* Unlike fossil fuels, water isn't destroyed by being used, but the way it is used has important effects on the environment. When water is taken from a river, used in homes or factories, and then treated and returned, river flows are more or less unchanged. But, when water is sprayed onto fields, lawns or golf courses, most of it takes the hydrological equivalent of a short-cut, EVAPORATING BACK DIRECTLY INTO THE AIR. This has damaging effects on the wildlife of rivers and wetlands because it removes the resource that is essential for their survival.

* *In developed countries, about a quarter of all the water withdrawn from rivers and underground aquifers vanishes in this way.* WITH WATER CONSUMPTION TRIPLING SINCE 1950, fresh-water life faces hard times ahead.

KEY WORDS

AQUIFER:
a layer or layers of porous rock, saturated with groundwater
GROUNDWATER:
water that moves through the ground instead of over it
WATER TABLE:
the level marking the upper boundary of the groundwater in any area

water used for irrigation evaporates away

Comparing thirsts

The world's thirstiest country by far is the former Soviet Republic of Turkmenistan, where 16,500 litres (3,600 gallons) are used per person per day – mainly on agriculture. This is about 1.5 million times the amount of water that each inhabitant would theoretically need simply to stay alive.

119

NO HIDING PLACE

* The oceans have been described as the final frontier of the hunting way of life. Until the 20th century, the hunt was finely balanced: finding and catching fish was an inefficient and hazardous business, and only a tiny fraction of the fish stock was brought to land each year. Today, modern technology allows fishing boats to move in with pinpoint accuracy, and as a result many fish stocks have collapsed.

spear-fishing does not have much effect on fish numbers

THE ONES THAT GET AWAY

Since the 1960s, world fish catches have doubled, but only about half of the 110-million-tonne harvest ends up as human food. One-quarter of the remainder is used to make fish meal, which is fed to animals. The rest is 'by-catch' – unwanted fish that are simply thrown back into the sea.

TAKING THE PLUNGE

* Fluctuations in fish catches are nothing new. In Sweden, historical research shows that over the last thousand years, good herring catches have followed bad ones in a cycle about a century long. Long ago, it is very unlikely that the fishermen had any effect on herring stocks – the cycle was much more likely to be one of the normal oscillations often found in nature. But, during the 20th century, HERRING STOCKS PLUNGED in a way that they had never done before. To save the species from extinction, herring fishing was banned.

herring

I'm going down!

cod

✱ As fishing methods have improved, this pattern has been repeated in many other parts of the world. *California sardines were first fished commercially in the early 1900s, and in the 1930s over 60,000 tonnes were being landed every year.* By 1950, hardly any were left. In the Grand Banks off Newfoundland – a major fishery for several centuries – cod stocks crashed in the late 1980s. So many ships had converged on the area that adult cod had no chance of escape.

FILLING THE GAP

✱ What happens to other marine animals when a formerly important species is suddenly removed from the scene? *In the case of the California sardine, another fish – the anchovy – seems to have swum into the gap.* Something similar happened in Antarctic waters when baleen whales were decimated early this century. The misleadingly named crab-eater seal – which actually eats krill and not crabs – benefited from the whales' demise, boosting its population to about 40 million – more than all the world's other seals put together.

✱ However, while this is good news for anchovies and crab-eaters, it is bad news for ocean life as a whole. By removing key species, fishing and whaling MAKE OCEAN ECOSYSTEMS MORE UNSTABLE, disrupting balances that have taken a long time to evolve.

Easy pickings

Compared to fishermen, whalers got off to a much earlier start in reducing the numbers of their prey. Commercial hunting of right whales began in the Bay of Biscay over 800 years ago, and, by the 14th century, Basque whalers were already having to search far afield for animals to catch. By the 1500s, they had reached as far as the Grand Banks off Newfoundland. Within the next hundred years, whalers from a variety of countries came close to eradicating the right whale from the North Atlantic.

mmm, fish and chips

121

GOING UNDERGROUND

* When the Gold Rush hit California in 1849, thousands of prospectors poured into the Sierra Nevada, anxious to get rich quick. Besides making fortunes for the lucky few, the Rush had another and much less desirable effect: almost a billion cubic metres (35 billion cubic feet) of mining waste were washed down streams and rivers, ending up in San Francisco Bay.

a group of shifty-looking prospectors

Just add water

People dig up about 3,000 billion tonnes of soil and rock every year. Some of this is used to produce metals, but an increasing amount is used in the production of building materials, including crushed rock, sand and cement. On average, Western Europeans – who lead the world in cement 'consumption' – get through nearly half a tonne a year per person.

RICH PICKINGS

* Metals make up about a fifth of the Earth's crust, so there is LITTLE DANGER OF THEM RUNNING OUT. Iron and aluminium are almost everywhere, and even scarce metals like platinum and gold wouldn't sound that scarce if the total stocks could be weighed. However, as the California 'Forty-Niners' discovered, there is a snag to this natural bounty. To get at anything useful, a lot of unwanted matter has to be got out of the way. The scarcer something is, THE MORE THIS WASTE ADDS UP, AND THE MORE ECOLOGICAL PROBLEMS IT CREATES.

there's plenty of gold, you just have to be able to get at it

most of the rock we dig up is used for building

✱ The waste from the '49 gold rush made rivers burst their banks, and smothered animal life once it reached the sea. San Francisco Bay eventually recovered, but other side-effects of mining can last much longer. *Being buried by waste is one problem faced by plants and animals in mining areas; being poisoned by it is another.*

DOUBLE STRIKE

✱ Mining waste often contains high concentrations of <u>HEAVY METALS</u>, such as copper and lead, which become 'mobilized' by rainwater when the waste is piled on the ground. The metallic mixture drains into waterways, killing freshwater wildlife. Smelting and refining also create pollution by releasing toxic substances into the air. At big smelters, this can kill vegetation for miles around.

✱ As long ago as the 1500s, the German metallurgist **Georg Bauer** – better known as **Agricola** – noted another effect of smelting: it has a voracious appetite for energy. *In Agricola's day, the energy came from wood, and it went into making iron.* Iron is relatively easy to extract from mineral ores, but aluminium, which was discovered in 1825, is fiendishly difficult. This is why aluminium smelting now takes up <u>1% OF ALL THE ENERGY USED IN THE WORLD</u>.

HALF-KILOMETRE HOLE

The increasing use of metals is responsible for the biggest man-made hole in the world – the Bingham Canyon copper mine in Utah, USA. It is 800m (0.5 mile) deep, and 4km (2.5 miles) across. The rock removed from the hole would fill the Panama Canal seven times over.

One tough grass

It takes a special kind of plant to survive on lead mine waste. In Wales, botanists have discovered that fine bent-grass has managed to adapt to this harsh environment, developing resistance to lead levels of up to 1% – enough to kill most other forms of plant life (and animals as well).

123

BRIGHT LIGHTS, BIG CITIES

* In the year 1700, only five cities had populations of more than half a million: London, Paris and Constantinople (now Istanbul) in the West, and Beijing and Tokyo in the East. A century later, this list of 'supercities' had only risen by one - Canton - and most were still compact enough to walk across in half an hour. Since then, cities have expanded even faster than the world's population as a whole.

New neighbours

The typical suburban patchwork of houses and gardens seems to suit some animals better than life in their original habitat. Racoons and foxes have both taken up suburban life, and suburban birdlife is sometimes richer than that in the countryside around. In the USA, one ground-nesting bird – the common nighthawk – has successfully moved into city centres, laying its eggs on flat gravel roofs.

STREET LIFE

New York, New York...

racoons

* In 1800, only about 3% of the world's people lived in cities, and even the biggest ones were small by modern standards. They had to be: the only form of transport was the horse. In ecological terms, cities were major blots on the landscape, but their collective impact was limited because they were few and far between.

* Today there are OVER 200 CITIES WITH MORE THAN A MILLION INHABITANTS, and over a dozen with ten million each. Instead of being a minority lifestyle, city living is rapidly becoming the norm.

URBAN ISLANDS

✱ Cities affect the environment in many ways. You don't have to be an ecologist to notice that they destroy natural habitats and generate pollution, but some of their effects are more subtle than this. Because buildings shrug off water instead of soaking it up, they speed up the flow of surface water after storms, increasing the likelihood of floods, and altering conditions for life downstream. They GENERATE THEIR OWN WEATHER PATTERNS, with more rain and cloud than their sites had before large-scale building began, and also slower winds. Cities also create 'HEAT ISLANDS', with average temperatures in the city centre often 3°C (5.5°F) warmer than the outer suburbs. This, at least, is sometimes good for wildlife: in some cities in Europe and North America, birds fly in on winter evenings to roost in the free warmth.

✱ *However, in the big scheme of things, fringe benefits like this don't add up to much for wildlife as a whole. Cities are centres of long-range consumption, pulling in resources from all over the world. The more cities there are, and the bigger they get, the greater the impact they have on the natural world.*

The city stakes

In the early 1500s, the Netherlands became the first country in the world to have 10% of its population living in cities. Today, the figure is about 90%, making the Netherlands one of the most urbanized countries in the world.

birds fly into cities for the warmth

RISE AND FALL

The term megalopolis was coined by the French geographer **Jean Gottman** in the early 1960s to describe groups of cities that coalesce into immense centres of population many miles long. The original Megalopolis was a city-state in ancient Greece, surrounded by walls and nearly 10km (6 miles) across. Ironically, its modern population is only 5,000.

starling

expanding cities

EXPANDING HORIZONS

✴ With cities and towns expanding at their current rate, the pressure on agricultural land is intense. Given this one-way change, will there be enough farmland left to support Earth's growing population? The answer - as so often with questions about resources - depends whose opinion you prefer.

FOOD 'IN THE BANK'

The world currently has enough stored grain to keep the global population fed for about 70 days. Despite improvements in agriculture, this is no better than at the beginning of the 1960s.

LAND AND FOOD

✴ *'Cornucopian' economists believe that land is an under-exploited resource.* About a quarter of the Earth's ice-free land is theoretically suitable for producing food, but at present <u>LESS THAN HALF OF THIS IS ACTUALLY FARMED</u>. On paper, these figures suggest that we could double our food supply simply by doubling the amount of land we use. If future improvements in technology and crop yields are then taken into consideration, the apparent shortage of land looks like no shortage at all: even with expanding cities, <u>THERE SHOULD BE ENOUGH TO FEED THE WORLD</u>.

✴ Most ecologists approach the question from a different angle. The amount of land under cultivation

there is enough grain for 70 days

today – about 1.5 billion hectares (about 4 billion acres) – has already created immense environmental problems. Some of these, like salinization, have ruined land that once grew crops. Expanding farmland into uncultivated areas is likely to make the environmental picture worse. *The ecological moral of the story is that, instead of looking for new land, we should protect the land we already use,* and CULTIVATE IT IN SUSTAINABLE WAYS.

MUST TRY HARDER

* The land-and-food question is complicated by the HUGE INEQUALITIES that exist across the world. Currently, the world produces just about enough food to give everyone what they need, but ONLY IF THE FOOD IS PERFECTLY DISTRIBUTED. That, of course, doesn't happen. *Food distribution is uneven, and so are diets.* If everybody in the world ate a strict vegetarian diet (a biological impossibility in the coldest parts of the world), global food production would feed us relatively easily. But, if everyone switched to a Western-style hamburger-and-fries diet, only half the world's population would get anything to eat.

* *In the past, improved productivity has helped to feed the world's growing population, but the task is becoming ever harder.*

Grain gain

Since 1950, world grain production has gone up by nearly two-and-a-half times, *but the growth in population has meant that production per person has gone up by a much less impressive amount.* In 1950, the figure was about 250kg (550lb) per person per year. Today it is about 300kg (660lb) – a level it first hit in the early 1980s.

it's impossible to feed everyone a diet based on meat

127

the 16th-century Dutch linen
industry was a major polluter

CHAPTER 5

DISHING THE DIRT

* Pollution is nothing new. In the late 1500s, Dutch linen-bleachers poured toxic waste into drainage channels called 'stinkerds', and, in the 1600s, coal-smoke made London's atmosphere so poisonous that several leading writers called for it to be banned. But, until the 20th century, pollution was mainly a local concern, affecting some places and leaving others untouched. Since then, it has become a problem that hardly anyone - or anything - can escape.

don't even try to escape!

In excess

Whether something is a pollutant or not is often a question of degree. Carbon dioxide, for example, is a normal constituent of the atmosphere, and is essential for plant growth. But, when large amounts of the gas are released by burning fuels, it becomes a pollutant.

NATURAL POLLUTION

* Humans don't have a monopoly on pollution. In nature, dead animals and rotting plants can contaminate waterways, while grass fires and volcanic eruptions pollute the air. In the sea, poisonous 'red tides', caused by population explosions of microscopic creatures called dinoflagellates, periodically kill millions of fish, leaving them beached and rotting on the shore.

* Over millions of years, living things have evolved a resilience to these environmental problems. What they do not have is any protection against the NEW AND VARIED KINDS OF POLLUTION found in the world today.

POLLUTION GOES GLOBAL

✱ Two technical breakthroughs – both in the mid-19th century – marked the start of the modern pollution age. One was the invention of the internal combustion engine. First constructed by the French engineer **Jean Lenoir** in 1860, it eventually created travelling pollution sources, on land, at sea and in the air. Another – made four years earlier – was the discovery of the first synthetic dye by the British chemist **William Perkin**. The dye, called mauve, proved immensely popular, and made Perkin's fortune. It also triggered a wave of research, as other chemists searched for similar substances. The new field of ORGANIC CHEMISTRY ultimately delivered not only new dyes, but also a vast range of solvents, drugs, pesticides and plastics. Some of these substances exist in nature, but most are wholly human creations.

✱ Today, the complete list of these organic chemicals runs over the ten million mark, and thousands of new ones are registered every day. All are tested for toxicity, but, because most have never existed before, their long-term environmental effects are unknown.

volcanic eruptions are one source of natural pollution

SAFE? HOW SAFE?

Fast-acting poisons are easy to identify, but mutagens – chemicals that cause genetic mutations – are a lot more difficult. The standard method used for picking them out, invented by the American biochemist **Bruce Ames**, uses a special strain of the *Salmonella* bacterium that is unable to divide and grow in the normal way. If these bacteria start to divide after a chemical has been administered, the chances are that the chemical can cause mutations – genetic changes that might lead to cancer.

KEY WORDS

POLLUTION: the disruption of living systems by the release of chemicals or other agents

THE DRIFT DOWNSTREAM

* If you had to invent a free waste disposal system, flowing water would be hard to beat. Water is a remarkably good solvent, and it's always on the move, whisking waste out of sight downstream.

Until the 1950s, most industrialized countries made the fullest use of this free service, and decades later some rivers are only just beginning to recover.

Getting the treatment

Sewage treatment imitates processes that happen in nature, allowing organic waste to be decomposed without harming fresh-water life. Things kick off with primary treatment, which sees the 'solid matter' settling out in a sedimentation tank. The liquid part of the waste then moves on to secondary treatment, where it trickles through filter beds or is stirred in aeration tanks. This allows bacteria to break down the remaining organic matter. The effluent is then treated with chlorine to kill infectious bacteria and viruses before it is finally released.

WATERBORNE WASTE

* *There are two main kinds of water pollutant – industrial and agricultural chemicals, and biological waste.* Biological waste has been poured or (more recently) flushed into rivers for centuries, often without any form of prior treatment. In 18th-century London, the Thames carried so much of it that an MP wrote a letter of complaint to the king, using river water instead of ink.

* Biological waste is 100% organic, so it soon breaks

sewage treatment plant

down. The trouble is that the organisms that do the breaking down – chiefly bacteria – need oxygen to do their work. If a river contains a lot of waste, most of its oxygen gets used up, and this has repercussions on river life as a whole. Sludge worms can survive in water that contains little oxygen, but more active animals – particularly fish – die out.

well, that's got rid of that

THE BIG CLEAN-UP

* By the 1950s, oxygen levels in the developed world's urban rivers had slumped to crisis levels – about 10% of their natural value. In London, the situation was so bad that a boat called the *Thames Bubbler* was used to inject pure oxygen directly into the water, an expensive fix that had only limited results. Fortunately, THE FIFTIES PROVED TO BE A TURNING POINT. Things could hardly get worse.

* On both sides of the Atlantic, the following decades saw the construction of many more sewage treatment plants. These allow the natural breakdown process to take place away from rivers, providing all the oxygen that the bacteria need. By the time the effluent is discharged, almost all of its organic content has been broken down. Treatment like this means that today's urban rivers, though not exactly clean, ARE AT LEAST BIOLOGICALLY ALIVE.

flushing the problem away doesn't solve it

SYSTEM OVERLOAD

Biological oxygen demand, or BOD, measures the amount of oxygen needed by decomposers (pages 28–29) to break down organic matter in water. The BOD for urban waste-water can be twenty times higher than the oxygen level in a river or lake.

injecting pure oxygen into rivers is an expensive way to increase oxygen levels

HIDDEN HAZARDS

* Despite great improvements in dealing with waterborne waste, no form of treatment yet devised can get rid of all the chemical contaminants that find their way into streams and rivers. These chemicals include fertilizers and pesticides, as well as a wide range of industrial by-products. Some are relatively harmless; others potentially deadly.

many ecological hazards are out of sight

MERCURY RISING

* In the early 1950s, the Japanese town of Minamata showed what can happen when industrial waste ends up too close to home. Fishermen and their families, together with cats and seagulls, began to show symptoms of severe poisoning. At least 50 people died, while many other sufferers of 'Minamata disease' were left paralysed for life. The victims had one thing in common – they had eaten seafood from Minamata Bay. Health officials discovered that fish and molluscs in the bay contained HIGH LEVELS OF MERCURY, which was traced back to effluent from a factory in the town. The effluent flow was stopped, but by then the damage had been done.

mollusc

* Heavy metals – which include mercury, cadmium and lead – are used in many industrial processes,

Shutting the stable door

Action against water pollution has traditionally involved 'end-of-pipe' solutions – in other words, action that deals with pollutants once they have been produced. In most cases, pollutant reduction is a much more effective way of dealing with the problem.

132

edible crab

but <u>ONCE USED THEY HAVE A HABIT OF ESCAPING</u>. Removing them from waste water is expensive and technically difficult. This explains why, years after the Minamata disaster, mercury still contaminates river water in many parts of the world.

we shouldn't have had those prawns

the people of Minamata were victims of water pollution

SINKING OUT OF SIGHT

✶ Waterborne waste doesn't always end up in rivers and lakes. Some of it <u>PERCOLATES THROUGH THE SOIL</u>, joining the hidden reservoirs of water deep underground. Because groundwater moves much more slowly than rivers, once it has become contaminated it usually stays that way for a very long time. *In eastern Britain some groundwater still contains traces of whale oil waste that escaped in the 19th century.*

✶ For wildlife, contaminated groundwater is less of a hazard than contaminated rivers and streams, but for humans it is much more of a problem. Groundwater is often used for drinking and irrigation. Because we extract so much of it, what goes down – whether it is whale oil, petrol or nitrates from fertilizer – sooner or later comes back up.

TROUBLE DOWN BELOW

Figures from the US Environmental Protection Agency show that groundwater in over 40 states is contaminated with nitrates from fertilizers. Over 30 states also have problems with contamination from pesticides, petrol residues and heavy metals.

contaminated streams are a danger to fish

mercury-free fish get it here

THE ADDITIVE EFFECT

* Minamata disease was a classic example of an alarming ecological phenomenon. Known as bioaccumulation, or biomagnification, it concentrates polluting chemicals in animals at the top of food chains. As a result, a pollutant that is relatively scarce in the environment can end up having a devastating effect on individual species.

MOVING UP THE CHAIN

* When inshore waters are contaminated by mercury, the pollutant becomes mixed with the seabed sediment. Worms living on the seabed take in the mercury along with their food, but they are unable to get rid of it as waste. In the sediment, the level of mercury is often very low – perhaps only a billionth part of any bucketful dredged up – but it SLOWLY BUILDS UP INSIDE the worms' bodies. Eventually, it can be 2,000 times more concentrated than in the seabed mud.

* This amount of mercury doesn't kill the worms, but it does put it in

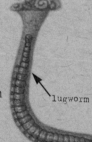

lugworm

I'm afraid you've got PCBs in your blubber

penguins contain high levels of PCBs

<u>AN IDEAL POSITION TO BE HANDED ON</u>. Each time it moves up a level in the food chain, its level is stepped up. Contaminated fish often contain five times as much mercury as worms, while seabirds often have eight times as much as fish. At this point, the mercury reaches life-threatening levels, which is why Minamata seagulls were affected by the disease.

SERIOUSLY RICH

✱ Bioaccumulation works with mathematical precision. Oysters can concentrate zinc by an 'enrichment factor' of about 100,000 times, and cadmium by 300,000 times. With organic chemicals – such as pesticides – the magnification effect is even more pronounced. When DDT gets into rivers, seabirds feeding on fish can accumulate 25 million times the level of DDT in the water itself.

✱ The more stable a pollutant is, the longer this magnification process goes on. A group of toxic organic chemicals called PCBs, or polychlorinated biphenyls, are a particular problem in water because they have a potential life of many decades. Unlike DDT, these industrial chemicals were <u>NEVER INTENDED TO BE RELEASED</u> into the environment, but they were, and they are still at large. Twenty years after their use was restricted they have spread throughout marine life in the seas, reaching as far as Antarctica.

Fatal fat

Chlorinated hydrocarbons – a group of chemicals that includes DDT – don't dissolve easily in water, but they dissolve very well in oils and fat. This is bad news for seabirds and ocean-going mammals, because many of these use body fat, or 'blubber', to keep out the cold. As a result, they store up chemical pollutants in unusually large amounts. Polar bears often contain high levels of PCBs (polychlorinated biphenyls) and so do penguins, despite the fact that they live in the least polluted environment on Earth.

polar bear

135

the average European generates half a tonne of rubbish

THROWAWAY TIMES

✱ Waste is an alien concept in nature, but it is an up-and-coming feature of the human world. Every year, the average European generates half a tonne of it, while Americans produce half as much again. With this amount of rubbish being thrown out, the days when waste could simply be dumped and forgotten about are rapidly coming to an end.

High-rise rubbish

The world's largest rubbish dump is in Staten Island, New York. It contains about 70 million cubic metres of waste (about 2.5 billion cubic feet), and gets bigger by nearly five million tonnes a year.

KEY WORDS

LEACHATE: liquid run-off produced when groundwater or rainwater soaks through soil or through buried waste, carrying substances with it

COVER UP

✱ In the 20th century, the history of waste disposal has been peppered with unpleasant discoveries and some hasty changes of direction. Until the Second World War, most industrialized countries got rid of municipal waste by dumping it in quarries or on low-lying ground. Once a site was full, it would often be LEVELLED AND COVERED with soil, and then used for farming or housing.

✱ This simple procedure ignored an important fact: RUBBISH IS NOT INERT. Once it has been dumped, the organic matter inside it starts to break down, giving off methane and other inflammable gases. At the same time, water trickles through it, carrying away a fetid mix of oils, dissolved chemicals and dangerous bacteria.

chemical waste leaking from dumps is toxic enough to dissolve the soles of people's shoes

✱ In the 1960s and 70s, a series of major pollution incidents showed that modern household waste is far too dangerous to be treated in this way. Landfill sites were redesigned so that <u>POLLUTED RUN-OFF, OR LEACHATE</u>, no longer had a chance to escape. Instead of being forgotten about once they are full, these high-tech rubbish dumps have to be managed and monitored for decades.

GASES AND ASHES

✱ The other traditional method of dealing with waste – setting it alight – has been beset by different kinds of problem. The first large incinerators, which were built in the early 1900s, burned waste at low temperatures, and generated large amounts of polluting smoke. By the 1950s, concern about air quality meant that incinerators went out of fashion. Two decades later, with landfill space running out, they came back in.

✱ Modern incinerators burn waste <u>AT VERY HIGH TEMPERATURES</u> – up to 1,000°C (1,830°F). This is hot enough to destroy anything organic, but it also vaporizes heavy metals such as mercury and lead. Despite improved techniques for trapping these airborne pollutants, it remains a dirty and expensive business – one that few people want on their doorstep.

The lessons of Love Canal

The 'bury-and-forget-it' approach to waste disposal was responsible for one of America's worst pollution incidents, in the town of Niagara Falls in New York. During the 1940s and 50s, over 20,000 tonnes of chemical waste were dumped in drums on the empty bed of a local canal. Later, once the waste had been covered, houses were built on the site. Over the following decades, the chemicals escaped, killing plants and animals, and even dissolving the soles of people's shoes. The area was evacuated, and the clean-up bill came to over $250 million.

$250 MILLION

137

WASTE THAT WON'T GO AWAY

✱ During life's long history, nature's recyclers - mainly bacteria and fungi - have evolved an ability to deal with a vast and varied menu of organic remains. What they have not managed to do, so far at least, is adapt to the man-made materials in today's household waste. Because they cannot be broken down, these materials are destined to litter the planet for generations to come.

human rubbish is almost everywhere

KEY WORDS

BIODEGRADABLE: capable of being broken down into simple inorganic compounds by living things (usually micro-organisms)

Added bulk

Biodegradable matter – which includes paper and cardboard, wood, food scraps and garden waste – often makes up over 50% of household rubbish. Plastics make up about 10%, but because their density is low, they form up to 25% of the waste's bulk.

DROPPING OUT

✱ The waste that people produce falls into two categories. BIODEGRADABLE WASTE, which includes leftover food, paper and cardboard, is organic matter which originally comes from living things. It can be broken down by decomposers as long as they are given the right conditions. NON-BIODEGRADABLE WASTE cannot be broken down in this way. Some of it disintegrates as time goes by, but much of it stays intact.

✱ Until the 20th century, this non-biodegradable waste consisted mainly of

it's twenty five years old

ceramics, glass and metals. All these materials are heavy, which helps to prevent them interfering with living things. Over the years, a huge array of objects made from these materials – from pots and bottles to coins, spoons and spades – have been abandoned or lost all over the inhabited world. Sooner or later, most have sunk harmlessly out of sight.

some rubbish can hang around for a long time

WANDERING WASTE

* With the invention of Bakelite in 1909, a completely new group of non-biodegradable materials came into existence. Unlike glass, metals or pottery, PLASTICS are light. Instead of staying put when they are dumped, plastic objects often float or blow away. Carried by ocean currents, some of them end up thousands of miles from where they were originally used.

* Waste plastic is more than just an aesthetic problem. Every year, thousands of marine mammals and seabirds are killed by becoming entangled in abandoned plastic nets and lines. Water animals can also be choked by expanded polystyrene, which breaks up into flotillas of fine particles that drift on the surface. In 1988, an international treaty prohibited the disposal of plastics at sea, but as a visit to almost any beach – no matter how remote – will show, WASTE PLASTIC NOW TRAVELS THE GLOBE.

Yesterday's news

Landfills often contain very low levels of oxygen, so organic matter dumped in them decomposes very slowly. Waste researchers have discovered that in some dumps, newspapers are still readable after 25 years underground.

fungi are nature's decomposers

139

UNCLEAN AIR

* Two hundred years ago, the poet Robert Southey described London's atmosphere as 'a compound of fen-fog, chimney-smoke, smuts and pulverized horse dung'. If he could visit London or any other major city today he would find that the smuts and dung may have gone, but air pollution is still very much with us.

air pollution has sources
big and small

Chemistry overhead

Primary pollutants are ones that are released directly into the air. Secondary pollutants are ones that form when primary pollutants react together. Many secondary pollutants are more problematic that the primary pollutants that produce them.

primary pollutants
go straight into
the air

SPREADING THE NET

* More than any other kind of environmental damage, air pollution works on a wide variety of scales. The smoke from a garden bonfire can create intense pollution locally, but its effects are negligible a mile or two away. The smoke and gases released by an industrial town need much more air to dilute and disperse them, so, when things get really bad, their effects can be felt a long way downwind.

* In Southey's time, this regional impact was where air pollution stopped. But, because cities have grown enormously, and because we burn far more fuel than people did 200 years ago, AIR POLLUTION NOW HAS A GLOBAL REACH.

particulates,
I think

INVISIBLE EXPOSURE

✱ When anything burns, it produces two kinds of pollutant. The kind that caught Southey's eye were PARTICULATES – specks of solid matter small enough to float in mid-air. Particulates are usually formed by incomplete combustion – partial burning that generates soot. Soot is a very visible component of air pollution, and on a local level it can be a serious threat to health. However, soot particles don't travel far. On a regional and global level, pollutants that can't be seen are much more damaging.

✱ These invisible pollutants are all GASES, and each has different chemical characteristics. Some, like sulphur dioxide, have a direct impact on living things, killing plants and animals outright when levels get too high. At the other extreme, carbon dioxide is completely non-toxic, although it can suffocate animals at high enough concentrations. But, poisonous or not, these gases have one thing in common: they are being released in unprecedented amounts, and some of them are now triggering climatic changes that affect the whole Earth.

AIRBORNE ESCAPE

If you leave the lid off a can of oil-based paint, the chances are that it won't be much use by the time you find it several months later. Paint solvents are just one source of volatile organic compounds, or VOCs, which create pollution simply by disappearing into the air. Other VOCs include spilled fuel, dry cleaner fluids and – most notorious of all – the coolants used in fridges and deep-freezes. VOCs all have a high vapour pressure, which means that they easily evaporate at room temperature.

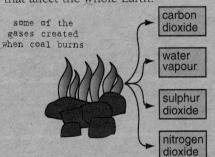

some of the gases created when coal burns

→ carbon dioxide

→ water vapour

→ sulphur dioxide

→ nitrogen dioxide

exhaust gas

ACID ATTACK

* Of all the gases that pour out of chimneys and exhaust pipes, sulphur dioxide was the first to be singled out as a serious environmental hazard. The indictments against it include killing forests and sterilizing lakes, but it has also managed to destroy some of the world's most treasured works of art.

Lost marbles

Marble and limestone are both attacked by acid rain. In Europe, acid rain has damaged many cathedrals dating back to medieval times, and it has also eroded sculptures in the Acropolis at Athens. Some of these ancient monuments have been covered in plastic resin to prevent further acid attack.

it's the sulphur dioxide that does it

sulphuric acid is one of the most corrosive compounds known

IT'S ONLY NATURAL

Thousands of miles from the nearest smoking chimneys, acid rain still occurs. This is because rainwater also dissolves carbon dioxide from the air, producing carbonic acid. The acid is very weak, but given enough time it can dissolves limestone to create caves.

CAN'T STAND THE RAIN

* Sulphur dioxide is highly soluble. Given the opportunity, it dissolves in atmospheric moisture to create sulphuric acid – ONE OF THE MOST CORROSIVE COMPOUNDS KNOWN. *In a concentrated form it dissolves metals and destroys organic matter on contact – quickly eating its way through skin.*

* Fortunately, the sulphuric acid that forms in the atmosphere is never as strong as this. But, even when it is very weak, its cumulative effect can be critical. FALLING AS ACID RAIN, it alters the chemistry of the soil, and has a particularly harmful effect

quick, lets get
out of the acid
rain, dear

on coniferous trees. When it is washed into lakes, the rising acidity can be lethal to fish, and equally deadly to the animals that they eat.

FALSE MOVES

✱ Ironically, the effort to combat smoke pollution in the 1950s and '60s actually made acid rain worse. In America and northern Europe, many coal-burning factories and power stations were fitted with extra-high chimneys to make sure that smoke particles were kept well clear of surrounding towns. These new chimneys not only dispersed the smoke; they also worked like launch-pads for sulphur dioxide, spreading it far downwind. As a result, regions like southern Norway and Sweden – which were not originally affected – found their FRESH-WATER WILDLIFE RAPIDLY DISAPPEARING. In parts of the world where the underlying rock is alkaline, this helps to neutralize acid rain, but in regions like southern Scandinavia, where the bedrock is chemically neutral, there was nothing to stop acid rain doing its worst.

✱ *Today, the picture has improved.* In developed countries, sulphur emissions have been reduced substantially over the last 20 years, and acid rain is not as potent a threat as it was. However, despite attempts to nurse them back to life, MANY LAKES AND FORESTS HAVE NOT YET RECOVERED.

How low can you go?

The pH scale, which measures acidity and alkalinity, runs from 0 (very acidic) to 14 (very alkaline). Battery acid has a pH of about 1, while water has a pH of 7. Many of the lakes in southern Scandinavia have a pH of 4.5. In Scotland, rain has been recorded with a pH as low as 2.4 – about the same acidity as vinegar – while in Los Angeles, the pH of fog has hit a low of 1.7.

where have all
the fish gone?

Norway's fresh-water
wildlife was seriously
affected by acid rain

143

refrigerator

Why the poles?

As yet, atmospheric scientists don't know for sure why ozone depletion is particularly bad over the poles. One possibility is that ice crystals in cold polar air provide microscopic working surfaces on which ozone breakdown can take place. Another is that winds circulating around the poles in winter help to corral ozone-destroying chemicals, which then set to work in spring. These winds are strongest over Antarctica, which may explain why ozone depletion is worse here than anywhere else on Earth.

oh no! we haven't got enough ozone left

HOLES AT THE POLES

✱ Ozone is the atmosphere's Jekyll and Hyde. At ground level it is a highly poisonous pollutant, and the most important ingredient in urban smog. But 25km (15 miles) higher up, in the stratosphere, the same gas forms a defensive shield that protects life on Earth from damaging ultraviolet light from the sun. In recent years, the shield has developed gaping holes.

ozone is the atmosphere's Jekyll and Hyde

UP AND AWAY

✱ The destruction of the ozone layer dates back to the 1920s, with the discovery of chlorofluorocarbons or CFCs. CFCs have some unusual characteristics, one of which is that they are REMARKABLY STABLE. After the Second World War, CFCs found a growing range of uses, particularly as refrigerants and aerosol propellants. Production soared, as did the amount of CFCs escaping into the air.

* At the time, no one thought much about it. CFCs were non-toxic, and they had never been implicated in any known environmental problems. But, in the early 1970s, the picture began to change. Two American scientists – **Mario Molina** and **Sherwood Rowland** – found that, although CFCs are stable in the lower atmosphere, or troposphere, they begin to break down when they reach the stratosphere. One of the products of this breakdown is chlorine, a substance that triggers ozone-destroying chain reactions. Their research suggested that within a few decades the ozone layer could disappear.

aerosols are a major source of CFC emissions

Why ozone matters

Ozone screens out UV-B, the most intense form of ultraviolet light. Increased levels of UV-B can cause skin cancer and cataracts in humans, and can also affect plant growth. UV-B does this because its energy damages organic chemicals, and these include DNA, the substance that controls living cells.

PRIME SUSPECTS

* Molina and Rowland's work was dismissed by the chemical industry, and many atmospheric scientists were unconvinced. But, in the early 1980s, evidence for ozone destruction began to appear. British scientists found signs of a hole in the ozone shield over Antarctica each spring, and in 1984 a satellite confirmed that the hole existed.

* In 1987, an agreement known as the Montreal Protocol laid down an action plan for reducing CFC use, and that programme is now well under way. But, because CFCs can survive for decades in the atmosphere, we face at least a 50-year wait before the ozone layer starts to recover.

KEY WORDS

TROPOSPHERE:
the lowest layer of the atmosphere, extending about 12km (7 miles) above the ground. It contains most of the atmosphere's moisture, and nearly all of its clouds.

STRATOSPHERE:
the layer of the atmosphere above the troposphere. It extends upwards to about 50km (31 miles).

THE GLOBAL GREENHOUSE

John Tyndall

* Long before humans started to affect the ozone layer, the British physicist John Tyndall (1820-93) discovered something unusual about carbon dioxide: it is transparent to light, but it blocks the path of heat. This property lies behind the 'greenhouse effect' - a phenomenon poised to create the biggest environmental changes ever triggered by mankind.

The greenhouse gang

Carbon dioxide is not the only gas that contributes to the greenhouse effect. Other 'greenhouse gases' include water vapour, CFCs, methane and nitrogen oxides. Methane is produced by swamps, livestock and decomposing waste, while nitrogen oxides come mainly from burning fuels.

greenhouse

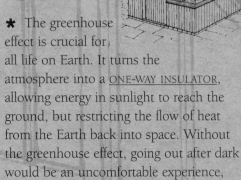

IT'S A WRAP

* The greenhouse effect is crucial for all life on Earth. It turns the atmosphere into a ONE-WAY INSULATOR, allowing energy in sunlight to reach the ground, but restricting the flow of heat from the Earth back into space. Without the greenhouse effect, going out after dark would be an uncomfortable experience, because, even in the tropics, an icy chill would set in as soon as the sun set. Average temperatures would be a bracing -20°C (-4°F), and most of the Earth's water would be locked up in ice.

* The strength of the greenhouse effect depends on the amount of carbon dioxide in the atmosphere – the more

put some more coal on the fire

climatologists can describe the weather of the past as well as the future

there is, the harder it is for heat to leak away. In pre-industrial times, the carbon dioxide level was probably about 250 parts per million. Today it stands at nearly 360, having risen by a quarter in 100 years. For something as vast as the entire atmosphere, this is an extraordinarily rapid change. This extra carbon dioxide has almost all come from one source: fossil fuels.

RUN ON THE BANK

* When fossil fuels are burned, they release carbon dioxide that has been buried for millions of years. This carbon dioxide is like a flood of money from some long-locked vault. Many climatologists now think that this extra carbon dioxide is bound to MAKE THE ENTIRE EARTH SIGNIFICANTLY WARMER in the century to come. If they are right, global warming will unleash a period of unprecedented environmental changes: changes that will be HARD TO PREDICT AND EXTREMELY DIFFICULT TO REVERSE.

ANCIENT AIR

Climatologists have been able to estimate carbon dioxide levels for the past 150,000 years by analysing bubbles of air trapped deep in Antarctic ice. This trapped air shows that the carbon dioxide and methane levels are highest during interglacials – warm intervals that punctuate Ice Ages. We are in an interglacial at present: the previous one was at its height about 130,000 years ago.

Northern exposure

Despite the general upward trend, the atmosphere's carbon dioxide level rises and falls every year. These annual 'wobbles' occur because most of the Earth's land – and therefore most of its plants – are in the northern hemisphere. During the northern summer, plants take up carbon dioxide. They release it when they die back in the winter.

147

MELTDOWN ON ICE

✱ During the early 1980s, when global warming first hit the headlines, opinions differed wildly about its possible effects. Some experts forecast a 4-metre (13-foot) rise in sea levels during the coming century, but by the late 1990s the figure had come down to 50cm (20cm). Differences like these highlight an awkward fact: with something as complex as an entire planet, no one really knows what impact global warming will have.

a rise in sea levels could cause a few problems

That one's here to stay

Despite recent scare stories, the likelihood of Antarctica's ice caps melting away in the foreseeable future is zero, because their vast size insulates them against temperature changes. Sea ice is a different matter, because it is very much thinner. A small sea temperature rise could dramatically reduce the amount of winter sea ice in the Arctic Ocean and around Antarctica.

ON THE ROCKS

✱ The knotty question of sea levels shows some of the problems involved. If the Earth warms up, <u>SOME OF THE POLAR ICE WILL MELT</u>, increasing the amount of water in the seas. At the same time, sea water will expand, contributing to the sea level rise. *Which will be most important?* In the 1980s, melting ice got the top billing, and expansion was overlooked. Today, many climatologists think that the real order of importance is the other way around.

✱ *If large volumes of polar ice do begin to melt, they won't all have*

no one knows for sure!

the same effect. Floating ice, which currently covers much of the Arctic Ocean, doesn't change sea level if it melts, just as a melting ice-cube doesn't alter the level of a drink in a glass. However, melting glacial ice – the kind that makes up ice caps – does raise sea levels, because it adds water from outside.

KNOCK-ON EFFECTS

✱ Predicting sea-level changes IS MADE EVEN HARDER BY FEEDBACK – processes that link one change with another. Ice caps are very good at reflecting light and heat, so, if they shrink, more light and heat will be absorbed. This will boost the warming effect, giving sea levels a further boost. But warming is also likely to increase cloud cover at high latitudes, reducing the amount of light and warmth reaching the ground. This increased cloud would produce more snow, paradoxically stepping up the rate at which glacial ice is made, and offsetting some of the extra melting.

✱ *This complexity means that future predictions about the world's sea levels – or any other factors influenced by global warming – have to be treated with caution. The further you look ahead, the greater the uncertainty.*

predicting sea level changes is a tricky business

KEY WORDS

GLACIAL ICE: ice in glaciers and ice caps, formed from compacted snow. Glacial ice can be over 4km (2.5 miles) thick, and can be thousands of years old.

SEA ICE: floating ice formed when the sea freezes over. Even at the North Pole it is never more than about 5m (15ft) thick.

Shifting shores

Looked at over the long term, today's sea levels are already high. Ancient coral terraces in New Guinea show that, during the last interglaciation about 130,000 years ago, sea levels were about 6m (19.5ft) above the present position, but, about 18,000 years ago, at the height of the last glaciation, sea levels were about 130m (425ft) lower than they are today.

149

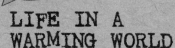

reindeer

LIFE IN A WARMING WORLD

✳ For reindeer living in the Arctic tundra, a temperature rise of a few degrees might not seem such a bad thing.

Similarly, few people living in cold places would turn down the chance of some extra warmth. Unfortunately, in a rapidly warming world, losers are likely to outnumber winners, as changing climate patterns affect the distribution of living things.

global warming is not as attractive as it seems

NATURAL CLIMATE CHANGE

Climate records suggest that the Earth is currently undergoing the fastest temperature increase seen at any time during the past 10,000 years. However, it isn't the fastest change ever known. Studies of fossilized insects show that, at the end of the last glaciation about 13,000 years ago, temperatures in northern Europe rose just as fast as they are doing today.

CASUALTY LIST

✳ Unlike humans, many plants and animals have very specific requirements for their survival – in other words they have NARROW ECOLOGICAL NICHES (pages 36–7). Local weather patterns are among the most important factors in determining these niches, and they are a feature that global warming is MOST LIKELY TO CHANGE. Because more heat energy will be stored in the atmosphere, the weather is likely to become more turbulent in the decades to come. Global rainfall will increase, but shifting air flows will mean that some areas actually become drier.

✱ Living things constantly adapt to change, and in the past they have survived some huge variations in climate. At the beginning of the last glaciation, trees throughout the northern hemisphere retreated as the glaciers advanced, only to sweep back again when the ice began to melt. But, each time changes like this occur, there are some species that fail to adapt, and they die out. THE FASTER SUCH CLIMATE CHANGES HAPPEN, THE MORE CASUALTIES THERE ARE.

FEELING THE HEAT

✱ At this stage it is impossible to say which species will be harmed by global warming, BUT THE LIST IS LIKELY TO BE LONG. Some may be directly hit by rising temperatures, while others will be affected in subtler ways. Polar bears, for example, do most of their feeding during the winter when they leave the land to roam the sea-ice in search of seals. In a warmer world, the sea-ice will form later each year, leaving them dangerously short of food as the summer comes to an end.

✱ For plant and animal life as a whole, global warming is likely to mean a further sharp fall in diversity, on top of the one that is already under way.

polar bears would be left hungry if their sea-ice hunting grounds were late in forming

Stepping on the gas

Because plants need carbon dioxide to carry out photosynthesis, increased carbon dioxide levels should mean that they grow faster. In theory, this increased growth rate could be one of the benefits of global warming, because it could boost the productivity of crops. But, in a warmer world, the overall prospects for agriculture are very mixed. Some of the world's most productive crop-growing regions – such as the American Midwest – could be badly affected by drought, which could greatly reduce harvests.

151

it's not our fault

A COUNTERBLAST TO WARMING

* According to the Intergovernmental Panel on Climate Change (IPCC), the world's average temperature may rise by about 2.7°C (4.8°F) by the year 2100. However, in climatology - as in economics - people often disagree about the importance of different trends. A small but vocal minority of climatologists dispute that global warming is really under way at all, while others agree that it is happening - but insist that it is not 'our fault'.

Frozen futures

Critics of the idea of global warming don't have to look back too far to find the last time climate data caused a scientific scare. In the 1940s, global temperatures peaked after rising by about 0.5°C (0.9°F) in about 60 years. Having reached this peak, they turned down again – a trend that carried on for the next 25 years. In the 1960s, just before the next upturn set in, many climatologists thought it quite possible that another Ice Age was on its way. Some still do.

OVER AND OUT

* Most of these disagreements stem from the fact that the Earth's climate record is notoriously difficult to analyse. In jargon borrowed from the early days of radio, the record consists of two kinds of data. One is the 'signal', or the part that contains significant information. The other is 'noise' – random variations which obscure the signal, sometimes drowning it altogether.

it's so difficult to analyse

climatology is a difficult science

* With climate change, SEPARATING THE SIGNAL FROM THE NOISE IS VERY DIFFICULT, and the shorter the period being examined, the harder it becomes. A five- or ten-year warming period can look very significant when it is actually happening, but in the long run it's the TINIEST OF STATISTICAL BLIPS. Greenhouse critics point out that over a single decade the Earth can look as though it is warming up, but over the century that includes that decade it can look as though it is cooling down.

are we to blame for heating up the Earth?

THE SEARCH FOR A CAUSE

* The second line of attack by greenhouse sceptics centres on the link between rising carbon dioxide levels and rising global temperatures. The current greenhouse consensus assumes that one causes the other, but there is always a possibility that the link is simply a statistical coincidence. If this is true, rising temperatures are being caused by something else.

* What might this something be? High on the list are variations in energy output from the Sun. These are known to occur, and they could account for climate change on a wide range of different time-scales. However, so far, the evidence is inconclusive. As far as the majority of climatologists are concerned, the prime suspect behind global warming remains the human race.

THE MODEL MAKERS

Unlike many natural phenomena, the world's overall climate isn't something that can be tested on a laboratory bench. The only way of assessing the impact of man-made changes to the atmosphere is to run computer models – electronic simulations designed to mimic reality as closely as possible. Greenhouse sceptics believe that many of these models are flawed, because they have to be constantly adjusted to keep them on track.

153

CHAPTER 6

SHARED EARTH

the population bomb

HISSSSSSS

✱ Global warming is not the only environmental issue to generate strong differences of opinion. Since the 1960s, when Paul Ehrlich wrote *The Population Bomb*, most environmentalists have taken the view that the Earth is becoming dangerously overpopulated, and that population pressure lies at the heart of most of the planet's ecological problems. Although self-evident to some, it's a view strongly opposed by others.

UNFAIR SHARES

Only connect

Among **Garrett Hardin's** other claims to fame is his formulation of the *'First Law of Ecology'*: where the environment is concerned, you can never do one thing without inadvertently triggering others. Some unintended consequences occur almost immediately, and are therefore easy to see. Others – like the impact of burning fossil fuels – can take several generations to become apparent.

✱ In 1968 – the same year **Paul Ehrlich** published his population primer – **Garrett Hardin**, another American biologist, published an essay called *The Tragedy of the Commons*. Using the imaginary history of a piece of jointly owned grazing land – the 'commons' of the essay's title – it examined the conflict between people's *short-term and long-term interests*.

✱ In the long run, Hardin wrote, the owners of common land all stand to gain if the grazing is kept in good condition, which means limiting the number of animals that are allowed to feed. But, in the short run, the returns

the owners of common land all stand to gain if the grazing is kept in good condition

look quite different. The person with the most animals fares best, and, in the scramble not to be outdone, the land gets overgrazed.

SHRINK TO FIT

✱ From a historical perspective Hardin's ecological parable has been disputed because, where common land has existed, rules have often governed the way it has been used. But the notion of common resources – and the damaging scramble to exploit them – has a direct bearing on environmental matters today. This explains why, three decades later, Hardin's *Tragedy* remains very influential. Instead of patches of pasture, today's commons include the soil, the oceans and the atmosphere overhead. They are jointly 'owned', and, in most cases, only international action can stop short-term exploitation producing long-term damage.

✱ So <u>AT WHAT POINT DOES OVER-EXPLOITATION BEGIN</u>? It is clearly linked to the number of people doing the exploiting, but beyond this, opinions quickly diverge. Some population experts have put the figure at about one billion – the level it reached about two centuries ago – but Hardin believes that even this is too big. *He has suggested that sustainable exploitation of the Earth's resources can only be achieved with a population of less than 100 million – a sixtieth of its size today.*

OFF THE DEEP END

For some 'deep ecologists', even a sixty-fold reduction in the human population would leave Earth with far too many people. Followers of this ultra-radical creed believe that the biosphere would be far better off without us – perhaps giving evolution an opportunity to generate a more successful form of intelligent life.

you can't bring that in here

there is a limit to how many people can benefit from common resources

the pill →

ROOM FOR MORE?

* Compared with global warming or water pollution, population growth is an intensely emotive subject. Almost all environmentalists believe that human numbers must be brought under control - a view shared by agencies such as the United Nations Population Fund. However, this idea attracts indignation and hostility from those who feel that overpopulation is a long way off, and that people should be free to reproduce as they choose.

Johnny, you're getting a little brother

PARTY POSTPONED

In October 1998, the UN Population Fund announced that the world's population is expected to hit the six billion mark on 12 October 1999 – six months later than previously expected. The reason for the postponement is a continuing drop in family sizes, brought about mainly by improved education and family planning.

BIRTH DEARTH

* During the last 50 years, improved methods of birth control have had a major impact on population growth in all the world's developed nations. In many European countries, population growth has gone into reverse, and in Japan and South Korea the population is expected to start falling during the next century. Of all the world's industrial countries, ONLY THE USA SEEMS TO BE BUCKING THE TREND. Its population is expected to climb from about 270 million today to perhaps 390 million in 2050.

← condoms

✻ About 50% of the world's women now use some method of birth control, but for religious and cultural reasons birth control is still a highly contentious issue. In the rancorous debate about birth control, environmentalists often stand accused of spreading myths and misinformation about the dangers of growing human numbers.

HAPPY FAMILIES

✻ Two of these 'myths', according to opponents of birth control, are that the world is running out of natural resources, and that it will soon run out of food. As evidence, the myth-exploders point to the work of Julian Simon and other 'cornucopian' economists (pages 106–7 and 110–11), who maintain that resources and food have no foreseeable limits. A third 'myth' is that overpopulation is already causing environmental damage. Here, the evidence comes from historical studies of land use, like one carried out in the Machakos district of Kenya. *In Machakos, researchers found that tree cover and cultivated ground have both increased over the last 60 years, despite a five-fold increase in population.*

✻ For the opponents of reproductive restraint, evidence like this confirms that there is no population problem. It's a position completely at odds with what most environmentalists believe, creating A GULF THAT IS VERY DIFFICULT TO BRIDGE.

some people argue that Africa needs more people, not less

Wanted: more people

Africa is often pointed out as a textbook example of what can happen when the human population expands very rapidly, putting resources under growing pressure. But opponents of the overpopulation thesis have argued that Africa's problems may stem from a shortage of people, rather than an over-abundance. According to this controversial theory, as Africa becomes more densely populated, services and communications will improve, raising the general standard of living.

157

we could borrow water from Alaska

Snaked Alaska

Rather than conserve water, Californians could 'borrow' it from Alaska. According to this plan, an undersea pipeline would snake its way down the American west coast, surfacing in the Sunshine State. An assumption of this plan is that Alaska's river water currently runs to 'waste' – a view that not all Alaskans would agree with.

TECHNOLOGY TO THE RESCUE

* In all the best disaster movies, the hero or heroine uses ingenuity to find a way out of a desperate situation. As fiction, it's a familiar scenario, but it's also one that is echoed by schemes to cure the world's environmental ills. Known as 'technological fixes', these schemes are all characterized by big-picture boldness, and a willingness to interfere with global ecosystems on a massive scale.

BEAMING DOWN

* A typical example of the technological fix is the long-established idea of using giant mirrors to beam extra sunlight down onto the Earth. This extra sunlight could be used to increase plant growth, so producing extra food. It could also warm up areas that currently experience long dark winters, making them more habitable for humans and opening up vast areas to farming. THE PROBLEM OF FEEDING THE WORLD WOULD BE SOLVED AT A STROKE.

giant mirrors could be used to warm up cold parts of the earth

those mirrors are certainly doing their stuff!

✱ It sounds an exciting yet practical idea. However, there is a catch. Like most other technological fixes, it is an exercise in engineering: the nuts and bolts of the scheme can be worked out down to the last detail, <u>BUT OF COURSE THE ECOLOGICAL CONSEQUENCES CANNOT</u>.

GLOBAL GLITCH

✱ What would happen if such a scheme went ahead? In the short term, the extra light would certainly increase plant growth. But importing light from space would also <u>CHANGE THE EARTH'S ENERGY BALANCE</u>, increasing the amount coming in, and therefore raising the planet's average temperature. Weather systems would almost certainly be disrupted by this extra energy, and so would the breeding cycles of many high-latitude animals. *The environmental disruption caused by the scheme could well cancel out its benefits.*

✱ The mirrors-in-space project is just one of hundreds that have been suggested. Others include schemes for diverting Russian rivers southwards from the Arctic to Central Asia, and a plan to reduce global warming by 'fertilizing' the oceans, making them soak up more carbon dioxide. They may look good on paper, but <u>NO ONE CAN SAFELY PREDICT WHAT EFFECTS THEY WOULD ACTUALLY HAVE</u>.

FERTILIZING THE SEAS

In the open oceans, low mineral levels mean that there is often very little plant plankton. In one recently proposed 'technofix' scheme, the surface waters would be artificially fertilized with minerals so plant plankton could grow. The extra plankton would remove carbon dioxide from the air, helping to reduce global warming. But the scheme would generate carbon dioxide because boats need fuel, and it would cause environmental damage because minerals have to be quarried. These drawbacks make its value difficult to assess.

THE APPROPRIATE APPROACH

* The shortcomings of big technological fixes do not mean that technology has no place in solving the world's environmental problems. Recent history has shown that in the industrialized world as well as the developing one, simple technological improvements can often produce quick and highly beneficial results.

let's line it with brick and clay

small improvements can have big results

Evolution and living filters

Wetland sewage plants imitate the natural purification process that takes place when water flows through a marsh. After travelling through a filter, the effluent trickles through a series of open-air beds stocked with reeds and other water plants. These plants absorb any toxic pollutants in the waste, while bacteria break down anything organic. By the time the water leaves the 'wetland', it is pure enough to be discharged into a stream or river.

ON THE BACK BURNER

* A classic example of this kind of improvement has taken place with the wood-burning cooking stove – a piece of technology that is vital to a large proportion of the world's population. Traditional stoves are highly inefficient. In an open fire, less than 10% of the heat generated by the fuel ends up cooking the food, while in the most basic stove, the figure is still only about 20%. Because the stove

a well-lined stove uses most of the energy it produces

open fires are
inefficient
cookers

wastes four-fifths of the energy it produces, four-fifths of the fuel is effectively thrown away.

✱ In Africa and parts of Asia, stoves like this have been used for centuries, and, in recent years, rapid population growth has meant that demand for wood has soared. The growing shortage of fuel has prompted a new look at the way stoves are designed. By adding a brick or clay lining, the <u>EFFICIENCY OF A STOVE CAN OFTEN BE DOUBLED</u>. Because the fire burns at a higher temperature, it can use a wider range of fuels. Demand for wood is reduced, giving forests a chance to recover.

COMING CLEAN

✱ This kind of simple engineering solution is an example of '<u>APPROPRIATE TECHNOLOGY</u>' – technology that is tailored to solve problems in the simplest way. In the industrialized world, appropriate technology can play a part in generating energy and dealing with waste. For example, 'wetland' sewage plants, which use water plants to clean up effluent, use less land and power than their counterparts, and produce cleaner water once their work is done.

✱ Appropriate technology may not be quite as glamorous as putting mirrors into space or rearranging the planet's water supply, but, because it is simple, it is easy to put into action, and it <u>CARRIES FAR FEWER RISKS OF UNWANTED SIDE-EFFECTS</u>.

BEAUTIFUL CONCEPT

The idea of appropriate technology or intermediate technology was launched by the German-born economist **Fritz Schumacher,** who wrote the best-selling book *Small is Beautiful* in 1973. Schumacher founded the Intermediate Technology Development Group, an organization that specializes in designing small-scale machines and production methods that can be used in developing countries.

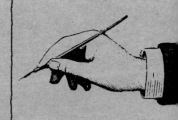

POLLUTION-FREE POWER

* Ever since electricity brought the gaslight era to a close just over 100 years ago, the business of generating power has steadily become more centralized, more complex and more polluting. In future, this trend is likely to be reversed, as power sources become smaller, cleaner and more diverse.

Chicken power

Biomass energy doesn't always come directly from plants. Animal waste, such as chicken manure, can be burned to generate power, and it can also be used to produce methane, a clean-burning gas fuel. In some parts of the developing world, cattle dung is an important alternative to wood. Once it has dried out, it burns well – and it doesn't need sawing up.

MAKING THE SWITCH

* Few would disagree that today's large-scale methods of generating power score low marks for environmental friendliness. They either contribute to global warming, or they involve substances that emit dangerous levels of radiation. Because we rely on them so heavily, they are certain to be with us for many years to come, but their near-monopoly is starting to crumble as a variety of less polluting sources come on stream.

* Clean – or almost clean – power is sometimes called '<u>RENEWABLE ENERGY</u>'. Strictly speaking, renewable energy does not exist, because used energy cannot be gathered up and recycled. Energy sources, on the other hand, often do renew themselves, thanks to the constant input of energy from the Sun.

HicCuP...

BURNING BIOMASS

✳ One of these renewable sources is BIOMASS, which in the energy trade usually means plant-based fuels such as wood, or alcohol from sugar cane. Unlike fossil fuels, biomass fuels do not have any net effect on carbon dioxide levels when they are burned, as long as the plants that produced them are replaced – something that doesn't always happen.

✳ *In rural parts of developing countries, biomass is often the only source of energy that is available,* but on a global scale its role is much more limited. It looks likely to stay that way. This is because there are several built-in disadvantages to burning biomass. *It is inefficient, because a lot of the energy goes to waste, and it can cause major environmental problems when the fuel is harvested from the wild.* Where the fuel is specially grown, it takes up a large amount of land that could otherwise be used for producing food.

SQUEAKY CLEAN

✳ For these reasons, most environmentalists doubt that biomass fuels will ever be a viable replacement for coal, oil or gas. Instead, the front-running alternatives for clean energy are the wind and waves, and – most promising of all – the Sun. Unlike conventional fuels, these do away with the need for burning carbon, eliminating the problems that this creates.

alcohol can be used to fuel cars as well as people

FILL HER UP

Brazil currently leads the world in using ethanol (ethyl alcohol) as a motor fuel, producing about four billion gallons (15 billion litres) a year. Ethanol is produced by fermenting the sugars in plants – a process discovered long ago when people learnt how to make alcoholic drinks.

KEY WORDS

BIOMASS FUEL: any fuel that consists of harvested organic matter, or substances derived from it. Biomass fuels include wood, straw, farmyard waste and ethanol.

163

windmill

A change of direction

The world's first windmills were built in Persia about 1,300 years ago. They had cloth sails that rotated on a vertical shaft, so they would catch the wind from any direction. By the time windmills became widespread in Europe, after the Crusades, horizontal shafts had been perfected, along with devices that turned the sails into the wind. Despite many experiments with vertical shafts, the horizontal version seems to produce the most efficient results.

waves have
energy that
we could
harness

WORKING WITH THE WIND

✳ Until the Industrial Revolution, wind and running water were the main sources of mechanical power. The devices used to harness them were surprisingly sophisticated, although most were also desperately inefficient. Nearly three centuries later, as the problems caused by fossil fuels mount, these renewable sources of energy look set to stage a comeback.

no wind..
no go
anywher

FREE AS AIR

✳ The wind may be free, but setting it to work isn't easy. The main problem is that its speed and direction are unpredictable. An effective windmill or wind turbine has to meet the wind face on, and its sails must be light enough to turn in a gentle breeze yet strong enough to withstand gales without being ripped to pieces.

✳ Traditional wooden windmills used a number of ingenious tricks to solve these problems, including gears that automatically cranked the sails into the wind,

and slatted sails that sprang open like Venetian blinds to let gales blow straight through. Today's wind turbines achieve the same ends through computerized control systems. With blades up to 30m (100ft) long, they are now beginning to rival fossil fuels as a viable way of producing power.

wind farms use computers to keep the sails turned into the wind

✱ In 1980, the total amount of energy generated by wind power was less than 100mW – enough to supply a small town. Since then, it has risen on an exponential curve, and is expected to reach a hundred times that amount during the early years of the 21st century.

THE NEW AIR FORCE

✱ *Wind power does have its drawbacks. The huge turbines are far from beautiful, and they can be deadly to birds.* But, to offset this, their environmental credentials are excellent. The same is theoretically true of wave-powered generators, but here the technical problems are proving much harder to crack. Compared with the wind, waves pack a knock-out punch: several test generators have been wrecked within a few weeks of being towed out to sea.

✱ *At present, wind power generates a tiny fraction of global energy use, while wave power generates next to none.* But some experts believe that with more research and investment the world-wide figure could be increased to 20%, reducing carbon dioxide emissions by over a billion tonnes a year.

PLUGGING IN

Although giant dams get the thumbs-down for being environmentally unfriendly, small-scale hydropower may play a useful part in meeting the world's future energy needs. In developing countries particularly, thousands of small dams that already exist could be converted to small-scale power production, meeting local needs without doing serious damage to the environment.

don't go near turbines

165

there's nothing like it

NOTHING LIKE THE SUN

* Clean though they may be, harnessing the movements of wind and water are still roundabout ways of gathering energy. For environmental and ecological reasons, it makes much better sense for us to move to the top of the energy chain and harvest energy directly from its source: the Sun.

the Sun is the fundamental source of energy

Sunshine state

Solar cells are made of thin wafers of a semiconductor – usually silicon. In bright sunlight, a typical cell produces a very small current, but cells can be linked up like batteries to boost the power output. One of the world's largest photovoltaic power plants, at Carrisa Plains in California, generates about 7,500 kilowatts of electricity. On a sunny day, its power output is about the same as 50 car engines running at full speed.

BRIGHT IDEA

* Until the mid-1950s, the only way to make electricity from sunshine was by using it to power steam-driven turbines – the same technology used to generate electricity from fossil fuels. Some solar power plants still work in this way, but the invention of the PHOTOVOLTAIC CELL in 1954 created an alternative way of turning sunlight into electricity. The advantage of photovoltaic cells is that – unlike thermal power-plants – they will work on any scale. A single cell the size of a postage stamp produces electricity just as efficiently as an array big enough to cover a football pitch.

solar panels

* After 40 years of research, photovoltaic technology still has a lot of catching up to do on other ways of generating electricity, but the efficiency of solar cells is constantly going up. *At the same time, the cost of making cells is coming down.* Photovoltaic electricity is still about five times more expensive than electricity from fossil fuels, but THE GAP IS CLOSING.

THE ULTIMATE CLEAN BURN

* One of the problems with photovoltaic power is that electricity is very difficult to store. A typical car battery, for example, holds only about 4% of the energy locked up in the same weight of petrol. Because so much of our energy goes into powering things that move around, any sustainable, low-pollution energy system must include an easily portable, clean-burning fuel.

* In the future, that FUEL WILL ALMOST CERTAINLY BE HYDROGEN, the lightest of all the elements. Hydrogen can be produced by splitting water with electricity. When the gas is burned, the process is reversed, leaving water as the only waste product. *Unlike carbon-based fuels, hydrogen has no impact on the greenhouse effect, and, with so much water on the planet, there is no danger that this ultra-clean fuel will ever run out.*

ELECTRICITY ON TAP

Electricity can be used to make hydrogen, but the process works equally well in reverse. In a fuel cell, hydrogen and oxygen are pumped into hollow cylinders of carbon, which are immersed in a conducting liquid. The hydrogen and oxygen combine to make water, generating electricity. Unlike a conventional battery, a fuel cell keeps running as long as it is supplied with fuel.

it runs on water

hydrogen from water is the fuel of the future

167

cars are the major source of pollution in America

LEAN MACHINES

✲ When using resources causes environmental problems there are two ways of trying to put things right. The 'business as usual' method - practised for most of the 20th century - deals with damage after it has been done. It's costly, difficult to organize, and often ineffective. A more recent alternative focuses on the causes of problems, and aims to minimize damage or prevent it altogether.

More for less

One way of measuring energy efficiency is to calculate the ratio between the amount of energy a country uses and its economic output, or GNP. This ratio is known as 'energy intensity'. The USA's energy intensity is about three times the figure for Japan, showing that Japanese industry needs only one-third as much energy to generate the same level of output.

DEATH OF THE GAS GUZZLER

✲ *This method of environmental improvement has scored some quiet successes in recent years. One example concerns cars.* Until the oil 'crises' of the 1970s, the average American car managed less than 15 miles on a gallon of petrol. The nickname 'gas guzzler' was richly deserved. Since the 1970s, car numbers in the USA have more than doubled, but at the same time fuel efficiency has increased. Today, the average American car goes twice as far on a gallon of fuel

as its counterparts did 30 years ago, so the AMOUNT OF EXHAUST GAS PRODUCED PER MILE HAS BEEN HALVED.

✶ This increase in efficiency hasn't stopped cars becoming the major source of pollution in America and many other parts of the world, but without it the environmental damage caused by cars would be even greater than it is now.

DAMAGE LIMITATION

✶ Using resources efficiently doesn't only reduce pollution: it often makes economic sense as well. With energy, research has shown that new power stations are often not the most cost-effective way of meeting increasing demand. Instead, it can work out CHEAPER TO INVEST IN MEASURES THAT REDUCE WASTE, which in turn releases more energy for doing useful work. Improved efficiency can also save money with raw materials, and with water used in homes and on farms. New trickle irrigation systems, used at night when less water evaporates, can reduce the amount of water needed to grow crops by 75%.

✶ But there is a catch. Improved efficiency can only reduce our environmental impact when the overall consumption is roughly stable. *If consumption is going up – as it is today – it merely stops things getting worse.*

THE BENEFIT OF AGE

The longer a particular technology has been in existence, the more energy-efficient it usually becomes. Light-bulbs have existed for over 100 years, and are now 50 times more efficient than they once were. Personal computers are still relatively new – and they waste most of the energy that they use.

watering plants at night saves waste, because less water evaporates

SECOND TIME AROUND

* Recycling waste materials is the closest many people come to doing something to improve the environment. It cuts down waste, it feels positive, and it is simple and easy to do. But how much does recycling actually achieve? The answer depends on the fluctuating levels of supply and demand, and on the differing lifetimes of recycled products.

recycling waste materials is a good habit to get into

Devil in the detail

'Environmental labelling' can often be misleading. Many products carry symbols that show they are made of 'recyclable' material, but this says nothing about how they are made. Some contain no recycled material at all.

what does this symbol mean?

RETURN TO SENDER

* *Recycling is a process that reduces a product to its original raw materials so that they can be used again.* It is most effective when there are clear cost benefits, so that MANUFACTURERS HAVE AN ACTIVE INTEREST in making it work.

* With some everyday materials, the potential savings are large. For example, it takes about ten times as much energy to produce a kilogram of aluminium from aluminium ore as it does to produce a kilogram by recycling – even though aluminium is one of the most abundant elements on Earth. For steel and glass the energy savings are

environmental labelling

60 per cent of
paper in use in the
UK is recycled

smaller, although they are still worthwhile.

✱ For paper and plastic – two of the most abundant components of household waste – the economics are much more finely balanced. At present, the cost of recycling these materials is often higher than the cost of making them in the first place, so a substantial proportion still gets thrown away.

PRIMING THE PUMP

✱ Most environmentalists believe that recycling is an essential tool in the campaign to reduce our global impact, and that THE RECYCLING HABIT SHOULD BE ENCOURAGED regardless of the short-lived ups and downs of the recycled materials market. According to this 'pump priming' argument, if enough people take part in recycling, it will develop a momentum of its own. As far as newsprint is concerned, there are signs that this is coming true. After several years in the doldrums, the prices for waste newsprint have risen to the point where collecting it makes good sense.

✱ Plastics are much more difficult to recycle because each type has to be dealt with separately if it is to be re-used. The output of recycled plastic is increasing, but, in most industrialized countries, plastic products still have less than a 1 in 50 chance of being melted down and used more than once.

Limited life

Glass and metals are ideal materials for recycling because they can be melted down and reused an unlimited number of times. Paper and cardboard have a shorter life span, because each time they are processed for recycling, their fibres shorten, reducing their original strength. In theory, many plastics can be reused indefinitely, but in practice, maintaining quality is very difficult. Even with careful sorting, different types of plastic invariably get mixed up, reducing their overall potential for re-use.

recyclable

171

creative accountant

CREATIVE ACCOUNTING

* In the past, the ups and downs of commodity prices have meant that recycling hasn't always paid its way. The same has also been true of other measures aimed at protecting the environment. Many environmentalists argue that this is because traditional accounting looks at a narrow range of costs and gains, and overlooks the bigger picture altogether.

Dirty secret

Taxing polluters is not always as straightforward as it seems. For several decades, many European countries have taxed petrol more heavily than diesel fuel on the grounds that diesel engines are more fuel-efficient. But diesel fuel has turned out to have environmental problems of its own: it produces microscopic soot particles when it is burned, adding dangerous particulates to urban air pollution.

it is not always economically worthwhile to recycle

COSTS AND BENEFITS

* The economics of paper and plastic recycling show how this kind of accounting works. When the price of making paper or plastic is calculated, THE ENVIRONMENTAL COSTS ARE USUALLY IGNORED. No one puts a price on the effects of logging, or on the impact of releasing polluting chemicals when plastics are made. On the other side of the equation, potential benefits are also overlooked. As far as the manufacturer is concerned, it's all the same whether a product contributes a lot to household waste, or contributes very little.

there's an added pollution tax miss

it's our pollution bill again

★ When all these environmental costs and gains are included in the calculations, the results are often very different. Something made of recycled materials scores well all round, because it reduces pollution and waste. If these advantages are reflected in the cost of the product, its low environmental impact may help it to succeed.

SETTLING ACCOUNTS

★ Environmental pricing is still in its infancy, but it is likely to become more important in years to come. It is part of a wider ecological principle – the idea that POLLUTERS SHOULD PAY. Since industrialization first began, the bill for environmental damage has been picked up by society as a whole, but when the polluters have to pay, it is much less likely that similar damage will happen again.

★ *In the campaign against pollution, big businesses are often identified as the villains of the piece. But ordinary consumers also play their part, and it is here that environmental pricing can make the most impact.* Many countries already have higher rates of road tax for owners of larger cars, and some cities have experimented with a sliding scale of charges to reflect the cost of dealing with household waste. If environmental pricing does become widespread, very few of us would escape.

the more waste you make, the more you pay

ROAD RAGE

Cost-benefit analysis is a well-established procedure in economics, but it's still relatively new in the field of environmental protection. One of the difficulties in using it is that people often disagree about how big particular costs and benefits actually are. New roads, for example, often damage wildlife habitats, but putting a figure on the damage is much harder than estimating the economic gain a new road is likely to produce.

that's just what I've been looking for

one person's waste products can be another person's raw materials

INDUSTRIAL ECOLOGY

* In industry - just as in natural ecosystems - the waste from one process can often provide raw materials that are needed by another. In theory, this can create industrial 'food webs', which generate far less pollution than each process operating on its own. At present, few of these industrial food webs actually exist, but they could become an important way of reducing the impact of industrialized life.

IT PAYS TO BE CLEAN

Between 1975 and 1995, the 3M Corporation estimated that it had saved over $750 million by designing pollution out of its production processes – a process known as 'industrial hygiene'. Many of the savings came from more efficient use of resources.

ONLY CONNECT

* Industrial waste may not sound like a promising starting point for an environmental clean-up, but in the right circumstances it can be exactly that. In the Danish town of Kalundborg AN INDUSTRIAL FOOD WEB HAS EVOLVED OVER the last 25 years, saving money and keeping pollution to a minimum.

* Kalundborg has a coal-fired power station that generates sulphur, a harmful pollutant in smoke. The sulphur is removed from the smoke, creating gypsum, a useful raw material. The

hygiene is good!

gypsum is used in a local factory to make plasterboard, and the board is dried by gas from a nearby oil refinery, which would otherwise be burned off as waste. Surplus heat from the power station, which would normally be lost, is used in a local pharmaceuticals factory, and also in houses in the town. Organic waste from the pharmaceuticals factory is used as fertilizer by the surrounding farms.

CLOSING THE LOOP

✱ Kalundborg's industrial food web is far from perfect because it is kept going by energy from fossil fuels. It also has several 'loose ends' – parts of the web where energy or materials still go to waste. LOOSE ENDS DON'T EXIST IN NATURE, which is why organic waste never piles up for long. To imitate a natural food web, these loose ends have to be tied up.

✱ On a small site this is rarely possible, but in a large industrial area there are many more 'species' in the web, which makes it easier for waste products to find a use. *Large industrial food webs also have another feature common in nature: if one of the 'species' goes bust – the industrial equivalent of dying out – there is a greater likelihood that another will be able to fill its place.*

hazardous waste can pile up if the law forbids it to be re-used

prickly pear

NATURAL ALLIES

✻ In May 1925, a consignment of small South American moths was taken by plane to north-east Australia. Their mission: to stop the advance of the prickly pear cactus, which had already smothered 25 million hectares (60 million acres) of forest and farmland. They were spectacularly successful. Within 15 years, the prickly pear had all but disappeared.

AN UNWELCOME ALIEN

The prickly pear cactus was introduced into Australia at some point during the early 1800s. It originally came from the American tropics — a region that is also home to its natural enemies, including the cactus moth. Cactus moth caterpillars chew their way through the prickly pear's paddle-like stems, making them collapse.

HELP, HELP, let me out I hate flying

moths were taken by plane to northeast Australia

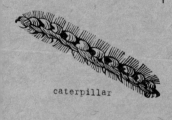

caterpillar

PRECISION ATTACK

✻ The prickly pear campaign was an early example of BIOLOGICAL CONTROL — a way of dealing with weeds and pests that uses their natural enemies to keep them in check. With the invention of synthetic herbicides and pesticides after the Second World War, biological control fell out of favour, but for environmental reasons it now has a promising future.

✻ The advantages are many. Unlike herbicides or pesticides, the living weapons used in biological control actively seek out their targets. Better still, they are very precise: they home in on one particular species, leaving others unaffected. They don't leave any toxic residues and, as their target species declines, their numbers drop as well. However, in many cases they don't disappear altogether, so the protective effect remains. *Australia's cactus moths are still 'on duty' over 70 years after they were first released, even though they are now quite rare.*

TOTAL CONTROL

* Biological control can work through chemical agents as well. In recent years, biochemists have identified many natural compounds that either attract insect pests, or interfere with the way they develop. Many of the attractants are PHEROMONES that guide pests towards potential mates. A pheromone can be used to lure insects into traps, and away from the crop they would otherwise attack. Development inhibitors work by preventing a pest maturing so that it cannot reproduce.

* *There are times when biological control isn't effective on its own – for example when a crop is suddenly swamped by a pest.* But, when it forms part of an INTEGRATED PEST MANAGEMENT SYSTEM, the need for herbicides and pesticides is sharply reduced. These reductions have already started to show in many developed countries, and in future years it is likely this pattern will spread.

KEY WORDS

PHEROMONE: any chemical released by one animal that affects the behaviour of another. Most pheromones spread through the air.

hey guys this smells great

insects can be lured into traps

Peter Pan insects

One useful method of biological control was discovered by accident, when entomologists found that contact with a particular kind of paper could stop some insects growing up. The paper was made from the timber of balsam firs. Research showed that these trees produce substances that mimic insect growth hormones, preventing them turning into adults.

endangered
species

SAVING SPECIES

✱ When Steller's sea cow was hunted to extinction in the late 1700s, few people were aware that one of the Earth's biggest mammals had gone for good. Two centuries later, much more is known about endangered animals, and their numbers are closely monitored. Since the 1950s, dozens of species have been reprieved by conservation programmes. Some are now off the endangered list, but others still face an uncertain future.

$25,000

A price on their heads

For some animals, illegal hunting for body parts is an even greater threat than habitat destruction. Rhino horn can fetch more than $25,000 a kilogram – a price that helps to explain the catastrophic fall in rhino numbers. The African black rhino, which has been worst affected, has fallen from a population of about 100,000 in the 1960s to just 2,000 today – by far the steepest decline of any large mammal in recent times.

BACK FROM THE BRINK

✱ One of the most successful conservation efforts started in 1951, when Hawaii's native mountain goose, or néné, had fallen to a total population of just 33. Three birds – one male and two females – were flown to a wildfowl reserve in Britain, in the hope that they could be encouraged to breed. The strategy worked. Nearly 50 years later, the descendants of these three birds are over 2,500 strong – ENOUGH TO ENSURE THAT THE SPECIES IS SAFE, and also to increase stocks in the wild. The California condor – down to 27 birds in the 1980s but now numbering over 70 – also looks as though it may have turned a

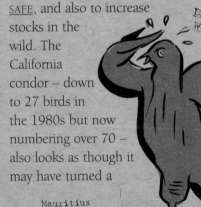

phew, th
was clos

Mauritius
kestrel

California
condor

corner, although as yet few birds have been successfully released into the wild. The Mauritius kestrel has had the closest escape of all. Down to just four individuals in 1973, its numbers now stand at over 300.

oh, if I must...

giant pandas are not very interested in sex

DANGER LIST

✱ Unfortunately, not all endangered species are this easy to help. Some – like the giant panda – are <u>SLUGGISH REPRODUCERS</u>, and have suffered the double blow of being hunted and also having their natural habitat destroyed. *Today's wild pandas, which number about 1,000 animals, are spread over more than two dozen pockets of bamboo forest, which greatly reduces their chances of successful interbreeding. To make matters worse, the pandas' food – bamboo – dies after it flowers, a form of mass suicide that takes place at regular intervals several decades apart. The last time this happened, in the mid-1970s, over 100 pandas starved.*

✱ Saving '<u>CHARISMATIC MEGAFAUNA</u>' – large, alluring animals like the panda – helps to focus conservation efforts and raises money. But, as environmental organizations realize, it is not an answer to the problem of endangered species: any long-term solution has to include saving the habitats in which they live.

IN THE RED

Since the 1960s, the World Conservation Union (IUCN) has published a set of '*Red Lists*' which identify species that are threatened or critically endangered. These lists, which now include over 40,000 species, help to target conservation work in areas where species are in imminent danger of dying out.

179

it's on the IUCN's list of threatened plants

PLANT RESCUE

* Compared with tigers, whales or pandas, endangered plants rarely make the news. But, from a purely practical angle, saving endangered plants could be one of the most important undertakings in the history of conservation. Plants contain an immense store of genetic diversity - one that we cannot afford to lose.

over 12% of the world's plants are in danger of extinction

Green fossils

dawn redwood

The history of plant collecting shows that rare species can stage a dramatic recovery when they are given a helping hand. One of the world's rarest trees, a conifer called the dawn redwood, was discovered in a remote part of China in 1944, millions of years after it was thought to have become extinct. Dawn redwood seeds were sent to botanic gardens all over the world, and the tree is now common in parks and gardens.

PICK OF THE CROP

* The IUCN's *Red List of Threatened Plants,* published in 1997, estimated that over <u>12% OF THE WORLD'S PLANTS ARE THREATENED WITH EXTINCTION</u>. Among this huge array of species are plants that could be the crops of the future, and ones that might provide useful medicines – if they are given the chance to survive.

* *Compared with animal conservation, plant conservation is still in its early days,* but botanists involved in this work do have some advantages on their side. One is that, unlike animals, rare plants can often be <u>PROPAGATED FROM CUTTINGS</u>, or even small groups of cells, allowing hundreds or thousands of plants to be produced from a single living specimen.

Another feature of plants is that their seeds are very durable – providing a lifeline that can save them from extinction.

PLANTS IN THE BANK

✱ <u>SEED BANKS</u> were originally developed by plant breeders developing new varieties of crops. In a seed bank, the temperature and humidity are kept at low levels, creating conditions that allow many seeds to survive for over 50 years. Because seeds are compact, thousands of species can be stored in a relatively small area, creating a dormant stockpile waiting to be brought back into life.

✱ With the threat of global warming, seed-collection has become an urgent business, involving botanists from all over the world. Collectors working for the <u>MILLENNIUM SEED BANK</u>, based at the Royal Botanic Gardens at Kew, in London, hope to have gathered seeds from 10% of the world's plant species by the year 2010.

✱ Collecting seeds isn't the same as preserving plants in the wild, but it creates a valuable breathing space during a time of rapid environmental change.

laburnum pod

apple seeds

sycamore seeds

a seed bank is one way of helping to preserve plants from extinction

AND THEN THERE WAS ONE...

Several of the world's most endangered plants are now so rare that only a single living specimen is known in the wild. These ultimate survivors include the St Helena olive, from the island of St Helena in the southern Atlantic Ocean, and the caffe marron, a plant from the island of Rodrigues in the Indian Ocean.

BACK TO NATURE

* Because habitat destruction is the leading cause of extinction, the best way to protect endangered species is to preserve their natural environment. About 6% of the world's surface has now been given some sort of protection, together with one complete continent - Antarctica. Many ecologists think that the total needs to be at least 10%, but it's a step in the right direction.

TOURISTS TO THE RESCUE?

Can ecotourists help to save the world's disappearing natural habitats? After a ten-year boom in this new kind of travel, the answer seems to be a qualified yes. In developing countries like Costa Rica, Kenya and Sri Lanka, money generated by tourism is helping to safeguard national parks and the species that live in them. However, ecotourists are too choosy to save a wide range of habitats across the globe. African savannahs gets lots of visitors: peat bogs get very few.

THE EXAMPLE OF COSTA RICA

* The amount of land set aside for wildlife varies enormously in different parts of the world. In North America the figure has reached 10%, but in the former Soviet Union it is just 1%. In Costa Rica – one of the flagships of conservation – an extraordinary 27% of the country is designated as NATIONAL PARKS AND BIOLOGICAL RESERVES.

* Costa Rica's experience highlights some of the successes and problems that come

WOW!

look

ecotourism raises money to conserve wildlife

with this approach to conservation. In this small country, deforestation has been savage. Without national parks, Costa Rica's tropical rainforest would have almost entirely disappeared. Today, the country's wildlife reserves attract thousands of ECOTOURISTS every year, who help to generate the money needed to keep the parks in existence. However, it isn't all good news for wildlife. Deforestation is still continuing, and the national park system is constantly threatened by demands for new land for farming.

DESIGNER RESERVES

✱ In recent years, research has shown that TOTAL AREA ISN'T THE BEST GUIDE to how well national parks or reserves work. Just as important is their individual size and shape. One large reserve will often safeguard many more species than the same amount of land divided up into several smaller units. One of the reasons for this is that the core of a large reserve is well away from 'edge effects' – the disturbances that come with human activity. Also, large reserves offer more opportunities for animals that need big territories: a pair of harpy eagles, for example, need at least 100 square kilometres (40 square miles) of tropical forest, while a male tiger can need ten times that amount. For these super-predators, small reserves are of little use.

KEY WORDS

EDGE EFFECT:
any disturbance on the edge of a nature reserve that affects the species within it. Edge effects include noise, pollution and intrusion by domesticated animals.

male tiger

Off limits

Antarctica is the only major landmass on Earth that has been successfully protected against species introduced from outside – mainly because very few outsiders could survive there. Under international environmental agreements protecting the continent, even introduced bacteria are banned.

LAYING DOWN THE LAW

✱ National parks and nature reserves help to conserve wildlife on a local level, but they can't solve the much wider problems of air pollution and climate change. Since the 1970s, a number of international conventions have been drawn up to tackle these and other environmental issues. None of these agreements is perfect, but several have already proved their worth.

environmental issues have to be addressed on an international scale

Protecting biodiversity

In 1992, over 150 countries signed the Convention on Biological Biodiversity at the Earth Summit in Rio de Janeiro, making it one of the most inclusive sets of environmental measures ever drafted. However, many of the Convention's recommendations are non-binding, and have been widely ignored.

CLEARING THE AIR

✱ The Montreal Protocol on Substances that Deplete the Ozone Layer, signed in 1987 and strengthened in 1990 and 1992, has been one of the most successful of these international accords. Under its provisions, over 90 countries agreed to HALT PRODUCTION OF OZONE-DEPLETING CHEMICALS BY THE YEAR 2006. Release of CFCs (pages 144–5) has now dropped sharply, although the ozone layer itself will take many years to recover.

✱ Compared with CFCs, carbon dioxide has proved a much harder pollutant to control. Most governments now accept that raised levels of carbon dioxide cause global

hyacinth macaw

who's a pretty boy then?

warming, but, because carbon dioxide is an inescapable by-product of using fossil fuels, IT IS HARD TO REDUCE GLOBAL OUTPUT. In 1997, the Kyoto Protocol to the UN Framework Convention on Climate Change called for industrialized countries to reduce their carbon dioxide emissions by 5% by the year 2010, which many environmental groups claim is NOT NEARLY ENOUGH. In 1998, negotiations in Buenos Aires showed that meeting the protocol's modest aims will be a difficult and contentious business.

PROTECTING WILDLIFE

✳ Other agreements have addressed the problems of acid rain, pollution at sea, water use and the traffic in endangered species – both dead and alive. The Convention on International Trade in Endangered Species of Wild Fauna and Flora, better known as CITES, came into force in 1975. It bans any trade in over 800 species known to be in immediate danger of extinction, and puts tough restrictions on another 30,000 that are potentially at risk.

✳ By any standards, CITES has been one of the BIGGEST SUCCESS STORIES in the history of conservation. Without it, there is little doubt that some of the world's most endangered animals – such as the black rhino – would already be extinct.

FREE TO TRADE?

The ivory trade shows some of the difficulties in making rules to save wildlife. In 1989 – following a huge decline in Africa's elephant population – CITES members agreed a total ban on ivory sales. But in the mid-1990s, Namibia, Botswana and Zimbabwe argued that the only way to save Africa's elephants was to allow small amounts of ivory to be sold, so that their elephants could 'pay their way'. Conservationists were – and still are – bitterly divided on this issue, but CITES members agreed to let the three countries sell ivory on a trial basis from 1999.

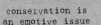

conservation is an emotive issue

PRESS FOR ACTION

* During the last three decades, politicians and industrialists have had to get used to some powerful new players in the field of environmental protection. Staffed by volunteers and financed by private donations, pressure groups such as Greenpeace and Friends of the Earth have scored some major successes in pushing forward the environmentalist agenda.

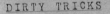
environmental protests are now common

DIRTY TRICKS

The Greenpeace ship *Rainbow Warrior* was sunk in Auckland Harbour, New Zealand, on 10 July 1985, shortly before it was due to leave for Muroroa Atoll in the Pacific as part of a protest against French nuclear weapons testing. An investigation by New Zealand police revealed that the ship had been holed by two bombs planted by French intelligence agents, triggering an international scandal.

GOING GREEN

* *Greenpeace was founded in Canada in 1971. The organization's original aim was to prevent nuclear weapons testing in the Aleutian Islands, but its scope soon widened to include many other environmental issues, such as chemical dumping and whaling.* Greenpeace's imaginative campaigns, skilful media management and rapidly growing membership made it increasingly difficult to ignore.

* Since those early days, pressure groups like Greenpeace and Friends of the Earth have become the cornerstone of the environmental 'establishment'. Once dismissed as post-hippy cranks, they are now major international organizations.

UNEASY PEACE

✱ With the dramatic growth of environmental groups – one estimate puts the figure for the US alone at over 6,000 – clashes between environmentalists and their critics are inevitable. With some issues, such as whaling, the facts are reasonably clear-cut, but with others they are not as straightforward as they seem. In the 1990s, for example, Greenpeace launched a campaign to prevent BP from sinking the Brent Spar, a redundant North Sea oil installation, in the North Atlantic on the grounds that it would pollute the seabed and set a precedent for similar dumping in the future. Although the campaign ultimately succeeded, most oil industry experts – and some environmentalists – still believe that dismantling these giant structures in inshore waters is more polluting than sending them to the sea floor.

✱ Difficulties like these are bound to continue in the coming century as a host of complex issues are tackled. But, as the French intelligence service discovered in 1985, when it sank the *Rainbow Warrior*, organizations like Greenpeace are a fact of life. Blowing up the opposition does not make them – or the arguments – go away.

protest is not just a hippy activity

KEY WORDS

PRECAUTIONARY PRINCIPLE: principle that holds that any new development that may be a threat to the environment or to human health should be treated as harmful unless it is proved to be safe

'Never doubt that a small group of thoughtful, committed citizens can change the world. Indeed, it is the only thing that ever has.'
Margaret Mead (1901–78), American anthropologist

FUTURE EARTH

* In 1900 it would have been difficult for anyone to imagine the phenomenal growth of mankind's environmental impact during the following hundred years. Today, at the beginning of the 21st century, ecologists and environmentalists have just as much trouble guessing how far - and how fast - that trend might be reversed.

who knows what the future holds?

DOUBLE OR QUITS

* This exercise in futurology hinges on how you read the human 'impact equation' (page 108). It's almost certain that the human population will nearly double by some point in the coming century, which on its own would double our environmental impact as a species. But the outcome will also be affected by changes in the way people live. If new technologies do manage to slim down our use of energy and raw materials, there is a chance that our overall impact will be reduced – but only as long as these new technologies are used world-wide.

I'm still looking for clues

piecing together the ecological evidence

WINNERS AND LOSERS

✱ Is this promising state of affairs likely to be achieved? Looking into the past provides few clues. Historically, humanity's environmental impact has fallen only when human numbers have suddenly declined – for example, during the 14th century, when an outbreak of the plague swept through Europe. There are few precedents for the opposite effect – improved environmental conditions when population levels are going up.

✱ For this reason, many ecologists believe that environmental protection will essentially be a holding operation until the human population reaches a plateau, say within the next fifty years. According to the optimists, after population growth has come to an end, a new era of ecological stability might be ushered in. For more pessimistic forecasters, this stable state sounds too good to be true.

WISING UP

✱ Whatever happens in the future, the last 100 years will have provided us with an unforgettable lesson: despite our extraordinary qualities as a species, we cannot escape the complex webs of ecological relationships that affect all life on planet Earth. In the chilling words of Mikhail Gorbachev, former President of the Soviet Union and himself an expert in unforeseen setbacks, 'ecology has caught us by the throat'.

MICROCOSMOS

Easter Island - famous for its enigmatic stone statues - vividly demonstrates what can happen when environmental damage spirals out of control. When Polynesians first settled the island, probably in the 4th century AD, it was covered with forest. Within a thousand years, the population had grown to over 5,000 and the forest was vanishing fast. By the time Europeans reached the island in 1722, food and timber were both becoming scarce. The last trees were cut down in the 19th century, and today the islanders - once self-sufficient - depend on the outside world for survival.

Mikhail Gorbachev